Creative Cloth Doll Faces

Creative Cloth Doll Faces

USING PAINTS, PASTELS, FIBERS, BEADING, COLLAGE, AND SCULPTING TECHNIQUES

BEVERLY MASSACHUSETTS

QUARRY BOOKS

Patti Medaris Culea

First published in the United States of America by
Quarry Books, a member of
Quayside Publishing Group
100 Cummings Center
Suite 406-L
Beverly, MA 01915-6101
Telephone: (978) 282-9590
Fax: (978) 283-2742
www.quarrybooks.com

Library of Congress Cataloging-in-Publication Data
Medaris Culea, Patti.
    Creative Cloth Doll Faces : using paints, pastels, fibers, beading, collage, and sculpting
techniques / Patti Medaris Culea.
        p.   cm.
    ISBN 1-59253-144-X (pb)
    1. Dollmaking. I. Title.
TT175.M457 2005   2004025594
745.592'21   dc22   CIP

ISBN-13: 978-1-59253-144-8
ISBN-10: 1-59253-144-X

10 9 8

Design: Peter King & Company
Cover Image: Allan Penn
Pattern Drawings: Roberta Frauwirth
Illustrations: Judy Love
Photography by Bob Hirsch and Allan Penn

Printed in Singapore

To Kieran, the new little doll in our family

Contents

"Every child is an artist. The problem is how to remain an artist once we grow up."

—PABLO PICASSO

Introduction

First impressions. What do we notice? Eyes? Mouth? Nose? The shape of a chin? The message in a smile? These same impressions are found in cloth dolls. The face is an important part of doll making. It reflects what you want your doll to be. It's who she is.

The face brings a doll to life. It should mirror the heart of you, the doll maker. For the cloth doll maker—whether a beginner or a hall-of-famer—the face of the doll is where memories begin. So how do you make your doll reflect the spirit and joy of its creator?

It is my hope that this book will help you bring a new level of creativity to your artistry. Quite possibly, your dolls' faces will do more than make people smile or reflect. I hope your expressive dolls will make hearts sing.

Basics

1

This book focuses on the doll's face. The tools needed for making the face are easy to find. Art stores, craft stores, and even fabric stores carry most of them, and none of them have to be expensive. You'll find many of the supplies in your home already.

The Basic Face Kit

mechanical pencil

ruler

eraser

fabric

watercolor pencils and/or crayons

fabric paints

pastels

colored pencils

seed beads in sizes 14, 11, 8, and 6

crystal beads

accent beads

drop beads

scraps of cotton, Ultrasuede, tulle, and other fabrics

cotton Lycra or other stretchy fabric

textile medium

brushes

The Body Kit

100% cotton fabric

cotton batiks

cotton Lycra or Doll Skin (stretchy knitted fabric)

Fairfield's Polyfil Stuffing

pipe cleaners for wiring fingers

16-gauge galvanized steel wire

thread to match fabrics

hand and machine needles

strong thread for sculpting

Hair Supplies

upholstery fringe

fabric

mohair

yarn

Dyeing Supplies

Jacquard's Dye-Na-Flow paints

Jacquard's Pearl-Ex pigments

Jacquard's Textile Paints

Jacquard's Lumiere paints

Stewart Gill paints in the Byzantia, Metallica, Alchemy, and Colourise ranges

Tsukineko's All Purpose Inks

wide, round, and flat brushes

The Basic Sewing Kit

sewing machine

sewing machine needles (sharps in size 10; metallic, embroidery, and top-stitch in size 12)

sewing machine feet (darning foot, open toed foot, among others)

sewing machine tools (for changing needles and cleaning bobbin area)

small bottle of Sewer's Aid

extra bobbins

hand-sewing needles (sharps, milliners, quilter's basting needles, darners, embroidery)

doll-sculpting needles (3" [7.6 cm] and 5" [12.7 cm])

beading needles in size 11/12 and beading thread

straight pins and safety pins

pin cushion and thimble

rotary cutter and cutting mat

cutting rulers and measuring tape

template plastic

scissors (paper and fabric)

pinking shears

hemostats (hand-held surgical clamps) or forceps

large and small finger-turning tools

stuffing forks

needle-nose pliers

wire cutters

seed beads in various sizes and colors

accent beads

crystals

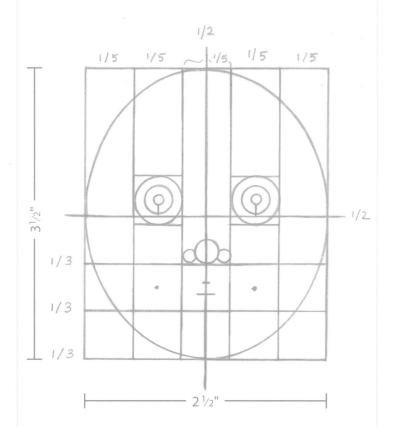

Clockwise from top left: grid, colored pencils, watercolor, paints

Getting Started

We can thank Albrecht Dürer for giving us a wonderful tool for drawing faces. Dürer was a draftsman, painter, and engraver who lived between 1471 and 1528. He came up with a grid method for drawing. He built a large wooden grid inside a frame, and put his model behind this grid. On a piece of paper, he drew a similar grid, and copied what he saw into his own grid. In this way he was able to create an almost perfect image of the model.

In drawing faces, this same principle can be used, only in our exercise we won't be copying a person. We'll create a new person. Refer to the illustration (below left) as you draw.

1. Using a ruler and a mechanical pencil, draw a rectangle 3½" tall by 2½" wide (8.9 x 6.3 cm).

2. Divide the rectangle in half widthwise and lengthwise.

3. Divide the vertical length into fifths (each unit will be ½" [1.3 cm] wide).

4. Divide the lower half of the rectangle into thirds widthwise .

5. Inside this rectangle, draw a large oval.

6. On the horizontal halfway mark, find each of the one-fifth units where the eyes will fit. Place a small vertical line through the center of each of these.

7. Measure the width of the one-fifth unit for one eye. This measurement will also be the height of the eye. Draw in a square, dropping the lower edge of the square about 1⁄16" (2 mm) below the halfway mark.

The basic grid for a face
(not drawn precisely to scale)

8. Inside this square, draw a circle. Inside this circle, draw a smaller circle. Inside the medium circle, draw a smaller circle. Before you detail the circles, you'll practice the eyes separately. When you're ready, you'll come back to this grid.

9. The nose is on the first one-third line below the halfway mark. It will fit inside the center fifth square. For now, draw a larger circle, centered above the vertical halfway mark, with a smaller circle on either side.

10. The mouth is on the next one-third line. This line is the base for the lower lip. To find the center of the mouth, measure ¼" (6 mm) up from the one-third line. Draw a small line. Another ⅛" (2 mm) above this line, draw another line. This is for the center of the upper lip.

11. The outside of the center of the mouth is exactly below the smallest circle you drew for the eyes. Draw a dot here, in line with the center of the mouth.

Now we'll practice each of the features.

The Eyes

1. Draw a large circle. Inside this, draw another circle. Inside the second circle, draw a smaller one.

2. The upper part of the eyelid starts slightly outside the larger circle, and curves up and across the top of the second circle. It ends on the outside edge of the larger circle.

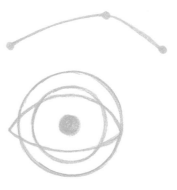

Preliminary eye

3. The lower part of the eyelid starts outside the larger circle, curves down slightly, touches the lower part of the middle circle, and connects with the upper eyelid at the opposite edge of the larger circle.

4. The crease of the eyelid follows the upper arc of the large circle.

5. Shade around the crease of the eyelid, and around the eyeball and iris, as shown. Darken the pupil, and erase a small bit for the highlight that is in the pupil and radiates out to the iris.

Finished eye

6. The eyebrows are slightly above the top of the eyeball. They start straight up from the inside corner of the eye, and stop just past the outside edge of the eyeball. The arch of the eyebrow is above the outer edge of the iris. For each eyebrow, draw a line, and then feather in the separate hairs, following this line.

7. The eyelashes start above the pupils, curve down slightly, and then curve up. Alternate drawing a short lash and a long lash until you reach the end of the eyelid.

8. The lower eyelashes are shorter and not as full. They start just below the lower part of the eyelid, and curve slightly down.

Practice drawing several eyes before drawing eyes into the grid of the face you made earlier.

The Nose

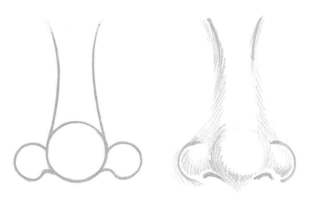

Draft (left) and finished nose (right)

The nose is probably the hardest part of the face to draw. On a doll that has a seam down the center of the face you don't have to draw a nose, but on a flat-faced doll you do. Here's the best way I've found to draw a nice nose.

1. Draw a large circle with one smaller circle on either side.

2. Toward the bottom inside of the smaller circles, draw in the nostrils. They are just two dots for now.

3. Measure the large circle, and double this measurement. Draw a line that length straight up from the large circle . This will be the bridge/base of the nose.

4. From the outside of the large circle, draw a line that curves slightly toward the base you just drew. Repeat on the other side.

5. Outline the flares of the nose. These are the two smaller circles you drew; you will just outline the outside of each circle.

6. Darken the nostrils, and shade in the rounded part of the nose.

When you are comfortable drawing noses, draw one on your doll's face.

The Mouth

Preliminary mouth

1. Draw a straight horizontal line. Draw a vertical line at its center.

2. At this center, draw a small circle. This represents the tubercle (sometimes referred to as the "milk bud").

3. On each side of this circle, draw a larger circle. Keep these larger circles closer to the center than to the end of the horizontal line.

4. Below these two larger circles, and under the horizontal line, draw an oval.

5. Starting at the center of the tubercle, draw a curved line out to the end of the horizontal line. Repeat on the other side.

6. The lower lip starts just in from the end of the horizontal line, curves down under the oval, and then curves up to just before the other end of the horizontal line.

7. Shade the upper lip and part of the lower lip, as shown in the illustration.

Finished mouth

Practice several more mouths, and then draw a mouth onto your doll's face.

Detailing the Face

Once you have a face you are happy with, outline the features with a brown fabric pen.

1. Outline the eyelids, the crease of each eyelid, the eyelashes, the eyebrows, the curves at the base of the nose, the flares and nostrils, and the lips. Erase all the other pencil marks.

2. Using a soft pencil, such as a 2B, add shading down the temples, around the eye crease, down each side of the nose, around the center ball of the nose, and around each smaller ball for the flares. Shade underneath the lower lip and a bit under the nose along the upper lip. This gives the face definition.

[step 1]
Basic face

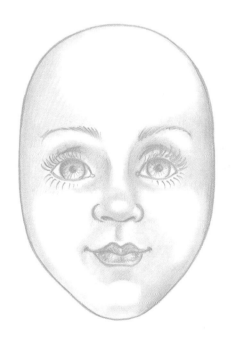

[Step 2]
Shaded face

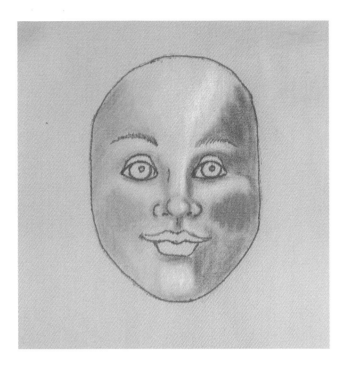

[Steps 1–4]
On the sample, the left side is blended but the right side isn't

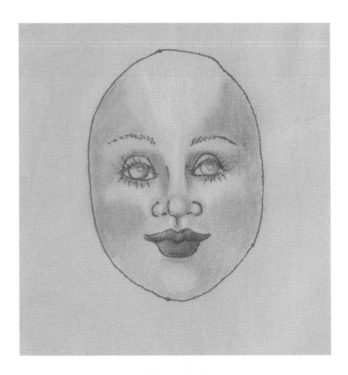

[Steps 5–6]
Eyes and lips are colored

Working on Fabric

It is now time to try drawing a face on a piece of fabric. Assemble a mechanical pencil and some colored pencils. You'll need brown, tan or beige, white, red, and colors for eyes and lips.

1. On a piece of flesh-colored cotton fabric, draw the oval for the face using the mechanical pencil.

2. Lightly draw a grid with a mechanical pencil. Add the features, and outline them with a brown fabric pen.

3. Add the shading, using a brown pencil. Follow the partially shaded face sample in Chapter 2 (page 25). Next, use a tan or beige pencil to start bringing in the highlights. Refer to the high-lighting guide (page 25). Lastly, use a white pencil at the high points of the face. Apply color to the cheeks. Don't be shy. When you blend the colors together, much of the pigment will rub into the fabric.

4. Once you have the shading, highlights, and cheek color, wrap a scrap piece of fabric around your index finger, and blend the colors by rubbing the fabric. On the sample (above left), the left side is blended but the right side isn't.

5. The eyes are next (see the sample, lower left). This time you'll need three shades of one color, or three different colors in varying shades (a light, a medium, and a dark). Use the lightest color to fill in the iris. With the medium color, follow the edge of the upper eyelid and one side of the iris. The darkest color is last. It actually starts at the inside corner of the upper eyelid and goes across the iris over to the other side of the eyelid. Darken down to the pupil with this color, keeping it along the top of the iris.

6. The lips are filled in with a medium color of red, peach, or rose. With a darker red, color the upper lip and one side of the lip that would be on the shaded side of the face.

7. At this point, seal the face. Iron it to set the colors, and then coat the face with a textile medium. Let it dry before doing the detail work.

8. Use a black gel pen to fill in the pupil.

9. Because you've been coloring a lot on the iris, its outline has been covered. Use a colored pen to outline the iris and draw in the rods that radiate out from the pupil.

10. Use white paint or a white gel pen to add a dot of white on the lighter side of the iris on the pupil and to color in the whites of the eyes.

11. Add a dot of red at the inside corner of the eyes for the tear duct.

12. Draw in the eyelashes. They start just above the pupil on the eyelid and curve down and then up. Alternate short ones and long ones. Stagger them to give a full-eyelash look. See the detailed illustration of the eye (right).

13. Use a red fabric pen to outline the lips and draw in the creases that radiate up on the upper lip and down on the lower lip. Add a bit of white to the lower lip. See the detailed illustration of the lips (lower right).

14. Feather in the eyebrows with a brown pen. Add black if needed.

15. Look at the face you have just colored. If you need to darken any shadows or lighten any highlights, do so now. Add eye shadow if you'd like. Iron the face, again, to set the pens.

These are the basics of drawing a face. The following chapters will cover several ways of coloring and creating faces. It is important to learn the basics, so when you move on from chapter to chapter, you'll know precisely where to place features— or misplace them, if you so desire.

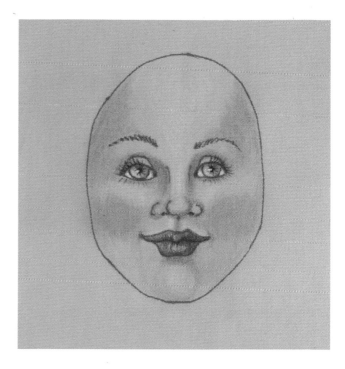

[Steps 12–13]
Detailing the face

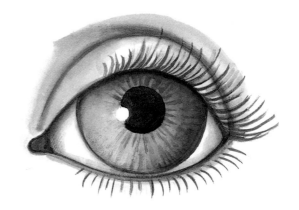

[Step 12]
Close-up of eye

[Step 13]
Close-up of lips

1/5　　1/5

1/2

1/3

1/3

Using Watercolors

 Watercolors are traditionally used on paper. I have found that using them on fabric is just as exciting, and the results are just as painterly. If a Monet-like look is desired, watercolor is the medium to use. It's also a wonderful way to get bright and beautiful colors.

There are different types of watercolors, including tubes, cakes, pastels, crayons, and pencils. They all work well on cloth. In this chapter, watercolor pencils will be used.

The doll featured in this chapter is a beginner doll with a simple, flat face. Because the head is attached to the doll after the face is completed, you'll have room for experimentation. There's no need to worry about making a face that is less than perfect. You can make several, and then attach the best version.

The Gallery section at the end of the chapter illustrates other artists' use of watercolor as a medium for bringing a doll's face to life.

Beginner Doll

Claudia is the perfect beginner doll. She's a good doll to use for learning watercolor techniques because her head is flat and is made separate from her body. Several heads can be made before deciding which one belongs on the body. This is a very simple pattern, allowing room for embellishments and fun. (The pattern pieces for the doll are found on pages 108–111.)

There's something familiar yet unexpected about Claudia's body parts. That's because they are copies of antique chair legs and bed posts. When I was puzzling over designing a beginner body type, I thought of a wall-hanging doll, and then noticed the legs on a chair and thought they looked like arms and legs for a doll. Remember, there's always inspiration to be found in your surroundings.

Claudia's clothing is made from pieces of lace that are dyed to match the overall color theme. Her hair is upholstery fringe, and her flowers are ribbons that are ruched and sewn together. She is simple and very elegant.

The head on this doll is sewn a bit differently than the doll shown in Chapter 1. Quilt batting will be used as the filler, with just a small amount of stuffing.

Materials

1 fat quarter each of 3 different cotton batik fabrics

one 12" (30 cm) square of flesh-colored fabric

thread to match flesh-colored fabric

strong thread for attaching arms and legs

one 6" (15 cm) square of quilt batting

stuffing

3 yards (2.7 m) of upholstery fringe

14" (36 cm) of 10"- (25 cm) wide lace or trim

1 yard (0.9 m) of 1½ "- (3.8 cm) wide lace or trim

1 yard (0.9 m) of flower trim for arms and neck

6 yards (5.5 m) each of 2 different yarns for knees

charms

four ½" (1.3 cm) round beads for joints

crystals or accent beads for centers of ribbon flowers

fabric paints in hot pink, sun yellow, and turquoise (Jacquard's Dye-Na-Flow works well)

mechanical pencil

fabric eraser

watercolor pencils (or crayons)

fabric marking pens in brown, black, and red

gel pens in white, purple, and black

3 yards (2.7 m) of ½ "- (1.3 cm) wide wired ribbon in 2 or 3 colors

Tools

pins

scissors

hand-sewing needles

turning and stuffing tools

soft brushes for applying dyes

container for water

containers for mixing dyes

stencil brushes

spray bottle

small plastic curtain ring

Making the Face

1. Trace the head pattern on the wrong side of your fabric. Double the fabric by folding it in half. Keep the right sides together.

[Steps 1–2]
Fabric, quilt batting, and slit

2. Lay a piece of quilt batting beneath the two layers of fabric. Machine stitch all the way around the outline of the head.

3. Cut out the head ¼" (6 mm) outside the seam line and clip the curves. Cut a slit in the back of the top layer.

AUTHOR'S SUGGESTION

To guarantee that you don't cut through both layers of fabric when you cut the slit, cut it before you sew the layers together.

4. Turn the head right side out through the slit. Place a small amount of stuffing in the head, just to fill it out a bit.

5. Draw in the features, using a modified grid method (page 13), with a mechanical pencil.

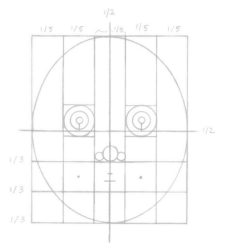

Modified grid method (see page 13 for full instructions)

6. Outline the features with a brown fabric pen. Erase the pencil marks.

7. Heat set with an iron.

   Now is the time to assemble your favorite watercolor pencils or crayons, a cup of water, a spray bottle, and stencil brushes.

Partially shaded face sample

8. Start the shading with a brown pencil. Color along each side of the temples, around the upper part of the eyelid creases, down the sides of the nose, under the nose, down the center area between the nose and the lips, and under the lower lip.

9. Use a lighter tan, cream, or peach pencil to add the highlights to the face. As the face curves upward, it catches more light. This is where the highlights belong. Refer to the illustration below for the placement of highlights.

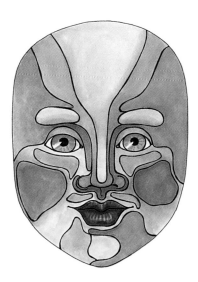

Highlighting guide

10. Use a white pencil down the center of the nose, across the forehead, on the chin, and across the cheekbones.

11. Use a rose or red pencil on the cheeks.

12. Blend the colors together with a damp stencil brush. (The stencil brush pushes the color into the fabric better than a regular watercolor brush.)

13. Use a yellow pencil to highlight the eye crease.

14. Use a purple pencil to deepen the shadows of the eye creases and gently darken each side of the nose.

15. Blend the yellow and purple together.

The face is just slightly damp now. It is important to not add any more water. Additional blending will be done carefully with a smaller stencil brush that is just slightly damp.

16. The eyes are painted using watercolors in three shades of one color, or three different colors in varying shades (a light, a medium, and a dark). With the lightest shade, fill in the iris. Use the medium shade to color around the top and sides of each iris. Use the darkest shade to outline the underside of the upper eyelid and shade down to the pupil.

AUTHOR'S SUGGESTION

I like working wet. I spritz the head with a spray bottle of water. As I start the shading, the colors will bleed out, and I'll know where to add the lighter colors.

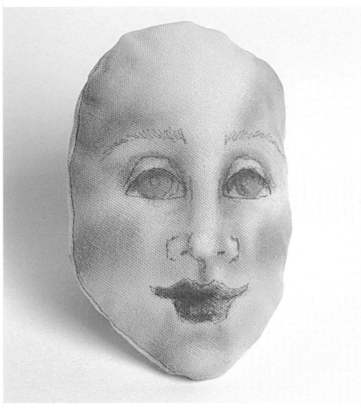

Face with colored eye, cheek, and mouth details

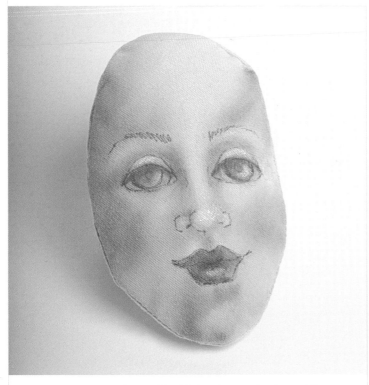

Face with blended and highlighted eyes, cheeks, and lips

17. Blend the colors with a small, damp stencil brush. (In the photo at left, only the left eye is blended, so you can see the difference.)

18. The lips are colored with two shades of red or rose, or any preferred color combination. Use the lighter color to fill in the upper and lower lips. Use the darker color to darken the upper lip, the side of the mouth that will be in shadow, and the lower edge of the lower lip.

19. Blend the colors with the damp brush. (Again, the photo shows blending only on the left side. You can see how the dampened brush smoothes out the colors.)

20. For final highlights, use a white pencil to lighten the center of the lower lip and the side of the iris that is catching the light. (On the sample head, that is the right side.) Blend with the damp brush.

21. Darken shadows and add highlights as needed, using the various pencils and the damp brush. If the brush gets too wet and you see a water-mark appearing, go over the entire face with the damp brush.

22. Let the face dry completely, then heat set with an iron.

23. Using a clean, fat, soft brush, cover the face with a textile medium. Let dry.

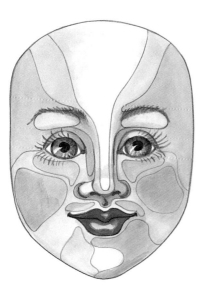

Detail the face with fabric pens

24. Detail the face with fabric pens. (Refer to the illustration above as a guide.) Once the detailing is finished, heat set again with an iron.

25. Sew the head to the body.

Finished doll head, complete with fringe and ribbon hair

Making the Body

All pattern pieces are templates, meaning you trace them on the wrong side of the fabric. After you have traced them, double the fabric with right sides together, pin, and sew, leaving areas open for turning where marked.

To make it even easier, you can use a light table to trace directly from the pattern pieces. Or, you can trace the pieces onto template plastic.

Once all the pieces are traced, you are ready to sew.

1. Begin sewing the body pieces, leaving areas open for turning where marked.

2. Cut out each body piece with pinking shears. Before turning, the top and bottom pieces of the body must be attached and sewn.

AUTHOR'S SUGGESTION

To make it easier to match the top of the head and the bottom of the body, use your fingers to make creases on the oval pieces.

---

3. Fold the Head Top in half lengthwise and crease. Fold again widthwise and crease.

4. Fold the Body Head Top in half from front to back and crease. You already know the other halves, as that is where the seams are.

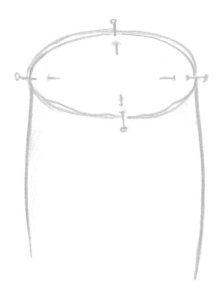

[Step 5]
Match the creases on the Head Top and pin to the Body Head Top

5. Match the creases on the Head Top with the creases on the Body Head Top. Pin them together.

6. Sew all the way around the head.

7. Crease the Body Bottom as you creased the Head Top. Pin it to the bottom of the body and sew, leaving areas open for turning where marked.

8. Cut small slits at the tops of the Arms and Legs for turning.

9. Turn all pieces right side out.

10. Fill all pieces with stuffing until they feel firm, especially the neck.

11. Close up all openings with a needle and thread, using a ladder stitch (see Embroidery Stitches, page 108).

12. Thread a hand-sewing needle with 1 yard (0.9 m) of strong thread and tie a knot at the end. Attach this to the inside of the Leg by the closed slit.

13. Sew the Leg onto the body at the hip by catching about ¼" (6 mm) of the leg fabric with the needle and thread, and then moving the needle over to the hip to catch the same amount of fabric there. Repeat to make approximately three connecting stitches between them.

14. Attach the other Leg and both Arms in the same manner.

[Step 13]
Sew the Leg to the body

AUTHOR'S SUGGESTION

Attach the arms and legs to the body before sewing the hands to the arms and the shoes to the legs. This way, you'll know which hand to attach to which arm, and which shoe to attach to which leg.

15. Thread a hand-sewing needle with 1 yard (0.9 m) of strong thread and tie a knot at the end.

16. Sew through the Lower Leg to attach the thread.

17. Use the needle and thread to pick up the large bead and then the Shoe. Push the needle through the top of the Shoe, and then back through the bead and into the leg. Do this one more time, and then anchor the thread off at the Lower Leg.

18. Repeat for the other leg.

[Step 17]
Attach the bead and the Shoe to the Leg

19. Attach the Hands to the Arms, using the same method.

20. Sew the Face to the top of the body, where marked.

21. Thread a hand-sewing needle with 2 yards (1.8 m) of strong thread and tie a knot at the end. Attach this to the nape of the neck, next to the Face.

22. Upholstery fringe is used for the hair. Start by sewing the fringe to the back of the neck. Tack down the fringe in rows, back and forth, to fill out the back of the head. When you get to the top of the head, sew the fringe across the forehead, and then tack it down in a circle on top of the head.

[Step 22]
Tack down the fringe to the neck and back of the head

Making Clothes

The lace trim will be colored to match the doll's theme. Jacquard's Dye-Na-Flow paints dye lace and trim beautifully without changing the "hand" of the fibers. Like any dye, these paints will bleed together to create new colors. They do need to be heat set; an iron will do the trick.

1. Cover the work surface with some type of plastic (garbage bags or plastic wrap work fine). Put some paper towels on top of the plastic to catch spills.

2. Wet the lace or trim, and squeeze out excess moisture.

3. Lay the lace on the paper towels and collect the colors you want to use. Pour these into small containers. (Ice cube trays work well because they have places to mix colors.)

4. Mix equal parts of dye and water. For pastel colors, add more water than dye. If you want brighter, more intense colors, add less water than dye, or add no water at all.

5. Brush one color onto the larger piece of lace or trim. While it is still wet, add the other colors. (On the larger piece of lace that makes the skirt on the sample doll, I started with yellow across the bottom. Next, I added pink, and last, turquoise.)

6. Color the smaller lace or trim in the same way.

Lace trim detail

7. Hang both pieces of lace to dry. Once they are dry, use an iron to set the colors.

8. With right sides together, machine sew the back seam on the larger piece of lace. Hand sew a running stitch along the top. Slip the lace onto the doll's waist, and finish by pulling the thread to fit. Tack in place.

Waistline detail

9. Cut the smaller piece of lace in half. One half is for the neck, and the other half will be cut in half again and sewn to fit the wrists. With right sides together, machine sew the back seams. Gather and tack the longer piece around the neck, and the two shorter pieces around the wrists.

10. Cut the flower trim to fit the neck and elbows. Tack in place.

11. Cut the 6 yards (5.5 m) of yarn in half. Wrap one piece around one knee and tie. Tack with needle and thread. Repeat for the other knee.

12. Tie charms to the ends of the yarn.

Creating ribbon flowers

Flowers for Her Hair

These flowers began with a mistake, through which —as we find so many times—a new technique was discovered. I was learning how to make silk ribbon roses, and instead of following the instructor's advice, I merrily sewed in my own way. When I pulled my threads, instead of a rose shape I ended up with a dahlia shape. (In my opinion, there are really never any mistakes in the arts.)

1. Thread a hand-sewing needle with 1 yard (0.9 m) of strong thread and tie a knot at the end.

2. Sew through one end of one of the ½" (1.3 cm)-wide ribbons. Sew in a zigzag, as shown in the photo. You'll need to sew five zigzags (going up and down five times), making ten segments.

3. When you reach the end, cut the ribbon and pull the thread to gather the "petals."

4. Form a circle by sewing from one end over to the other end, and pull the thread tight.

5. Flatten the ribbon "petals" and tack in place.

6. Sew the flower to the doll's head, and then sew a crystal or accent bead in the center of the flower.

7. Make as many of these flowers as you want. They can go in the doll's hair, on her waist, and on her shoes.

Finishing the Doll

Sew a small plastic ring to the top of her back. Now she's ready to be hung wherever you have a place that needs some perpetual flowers and a friendly face.

Queen of Congo Square

KRIS KNUTZEN

The artist writes:

Congo Square is a stage at the New Orleans Jazz and Heritage Festival. While attending the Festival, my ideas for the doll started developing. When I got back to Fairbanks, Alaska, and made her, I just knew she would hang out on that stage and never come home, if she had the opportunity.

To begin the doll, I used Patti's grafting-of-the-head technique. Because I used a brown fabric, I outlined the features in black, rather than the usual brown. After dampening the head with water, I began by shading with a dark umber. Next I used terra cotta, and then orange chrome. I overlapped the colors as I went. The dark umber went under the eyelids, down the sides of the nose, between the upper lips and nose, and in a circle at the top of the chin. I used my thumb to blend the colors into the fabric.

The cheeks are deep vermillion, crimson red, and magenta. Straw yellow was used on the forehead, the bridge of the nose, around the flare of the nose, and under the eyebrows. I blended with my thumb as I went.

By now the face was slightly damp, so I colored the eyes and lips. Lastly, I used white to add highlights to the inside of the eyes, the lips, under the eyebrows, and on the chin. When the face was dry, I did the whole process again, except for the eyes and lips. This time I used a damp brush to blend the colors. After the face had dried a second time, I sealed it with Delta Creamcoat Textile Medium.

Practice makes perfect. Oftentimes a mistake can turn into something really cool. Don't be afraid to experiment.

Sakari

SHASHI NAYAGAM

The artist writes:

The first thing I did, after drawing the features, was wet the face lightly and cover it with ochre, light brown, and flesh color, blending as I went with a stencil brush. Next, using purple and brown, I shaded the eye sockets, the sides of the nose, the nostrils, and the lips. The shadows were made deeper by adding dark brown and grey. I looked in a mirror to see where shadows needed to be darker or lighter.

The cheeks were blushed with a light red, and blended with the stencil brush. Next, I used white to highlight the cheekbones and the bridge, ball, and flares of the nose. As I worked with the white, I blended it with the brush.

Using my own eyes as a guide, I outlined the irises with a brown pen, and then colored them with light green, light yellow, dark green, and brown. For the lips, I used dark red for the upper lip, and light red for the lower lip.

Finally, I did the eyebrows with a fine gel pen, went over the rim of the eyelid with black, and gave just a hint of eyelashes. In reality, you can never see eyelashes clearly, but if you prefer outrageous eyelashes, go for it!

The Journey of Love

SHERRY GOSHON

The artist writes:

Creating faces is my all-time favorite thing to do. Since I was a child, I've drawn faces on all my notebooks, papers, you name it.

This doll was made of white muslin. For the face, I dyed the muslin tan. When it was dry, I used Derwent water-color pencils. First, I drew the basic face using a pencil, and then I started by coloring the way you would in a coloring book.

When I use watercolors, I start with the lightest colors, and then I come back and add shading. The eyes and lips were done first, using the lightest colors. I then used a darker shade for the upper lip and for the sides of the irises that are in shadow. Next, I added shading under the eyes, lips, and nose. I find it best to work from a photograph or pictures from magazines. They are excellent references for shading and highlights.

When the face was dry, I used brown and black Pigma pens to outline the eyes, the nostrils, the flares of the nose, and the lips. When the face had set overnight, I used a damp paint brush to blend my colors. Then I sprayed the face with a matte finish. This is a bit different from how most people do it, but it's how I do all my watercolor faces.

Solstice

ANGELA JARECKI

The artist writes:

In making Solstice, I wanted to capture the warmth and whimsy of a summer day. I chose yellows and reds, with just a bit of purple thrown in for my color scheme.

When I use watercolor pencils, I start with a pencil color that is only slightly darker than the fabric color. First, I lay in the shadowed areas, such as the cavity of the eyes, the side of the nose, and under the lips. I gradually darken the shadows, using a pencil that is a shade or two darker than the first color.

Within the shadows, I add a deep, cool color, such as blue or purple. Solstice has purple in her costuming, so I chose to use purple for the shadows to pull the colors from the costume into the face.

Next, I layer a bit of brown pencil into the shadows to blend them with the medium-tone areas of the doll's face. For the lips, I use the cool color that I chose for the shadow to lightly color the top lip, and then add a warmer lip color over that. The bottom lip is usually a warmer, orange-red color. The warmer color makes the lip look as if it comes forward in space. For the white of the eye, I use a medium gray toward the top of the eye, and white near the bottom.

To get the deep black of the iris, I wet the watercolor pencil itself. Wetting the pencils gives you a really rich, deep color.

When the face is almost finished, I lightly mist it with a matte fixative. After the fixative is completely dry, I go back in and add highlights to the eyes, lips, and cheeks. The fixative gives a nice tooth to the material, and the light colors hold very well to this foundation.

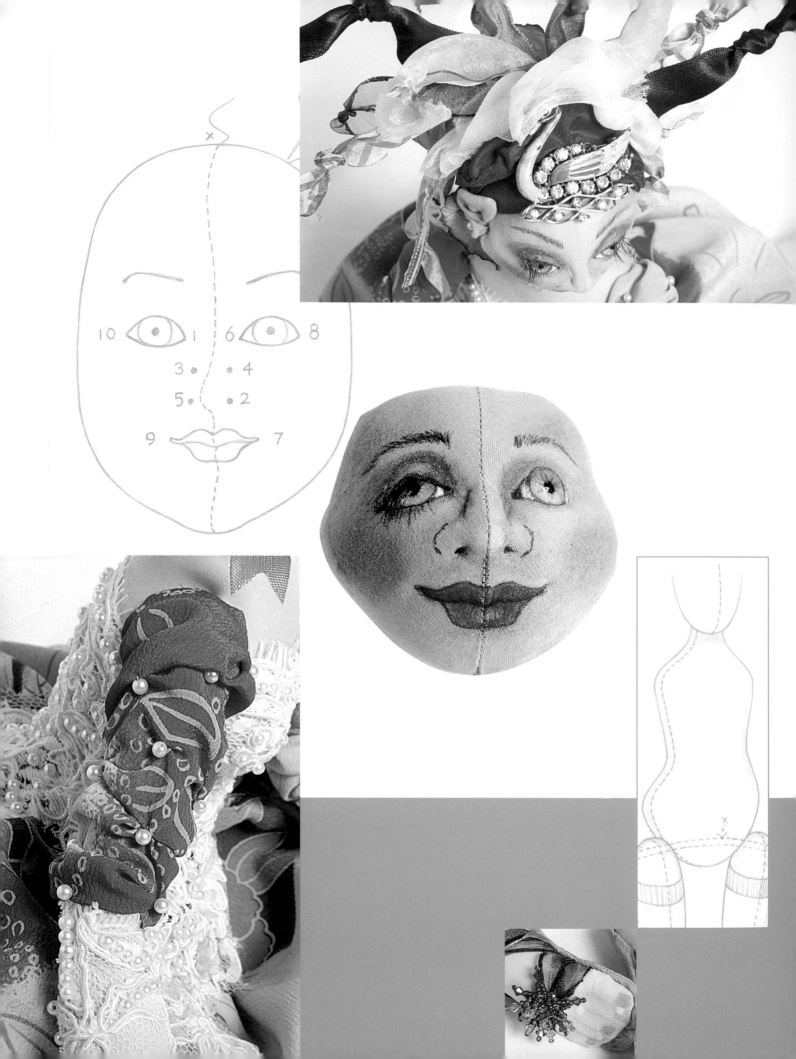

Sculpting the Head

3

The art of sculpting cloth doll faces has been around for centuries. In the late 1960s, the use of nylon stockings was introduced. There are some incredible doll artists who work in this medium. Another popular material is stretch fiber, which is similar to T-shirt fabric. In this chapter, I'll introduce you to sculpting with 100% cotton fabric. If cut and sewn with the right technique, 100% cotton offers results much like those you would expect from nylon or stretch fiber.

Intermediate Doll

Tania is an elf princess who is getting ready for a grand affair. She is made with the second body pattern and the #2 face pattern (pages 112–115). The body and clothing are very simple to put together, so that you can spend your time learning the sculpting and coloring techniques for the head.

Materials

1/4 yard (23 cm) 100% cotton fabric in skin tones

one 12-inch (30 cm) square cotton knit (a T-shirt will work great)

thread to match the fabric

mechanical pencil

strong thread for sculpting, in colors to match the fabric; button, carpet, and upholstery thread work great

stuffing

7 pipe cleaners

colored pencils in sienna brown, beige, white, carmine red, scarlet lake, lavender, canary yellow, apple green, peacock blue, process red, and Mediterranean blue

fabric pens in brown, black, red, blue, and purple

white gel pen, or white acrylic paint and a small brush

Ultimate Glitter Gel pens in pink, blue, orange, and violet

Jacquard's Lumiere paint in Halo Pink Gold, or other metallic fabric paint

Tsukineko's Fantastix for blending, or a small blending stick

a piece of bridal lace; it can have sequins and beads

pearl-colored beads, size 8, to match the bridal lace

light-colored beading thread

1/4 yard (23 cm) each of 4 different colors of silk, or silklike fabric (the sample doll uses dupioni, crinkle crepe de chine, silk gauze, and a poly/silk blend)

thread to match the silk

1 stocking from a pair of knee-hi's

1 small container of false eyelashes (can be found at drugstores)

textile medium for fixing face

brooch or antique pin for her headpiece

various ribbons in colors to match her skirt; these ribbons can be from 1/4" (6 mm) to 1" (2.5 cm) wide. You will need 3 yards (2.7 m) of each color.

silk ribbons, each 1/3" (7 mm) wide and 1 yard (0.9 m) long, in 3 different colors

12-inch (30 cm) square of craft felt

Tacky Glue (or white glue)

Tools

toothpicks

3" (7.6 cm) doll sculpting needle

turning and stuffing tools

beading needle

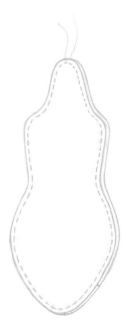

[Step 2]
Sewing of back, Seam #4

[Step 4]
Sewing front to back

Instructions

1. Trace the head, ears, arms, hands, legs, breasts, and body pieces on the wrong side of the flesh-colored cotton (see pattern, pages 112–115). Remember—you'll need to trace two pieces each for the ears, arms, hands, and legs.

AUTHOR'S SUGGESTION

If you can't find really good-quality cotton for the body, use a cotton bed sheet that is made of 100% Egyptian or pima cotton.

2. Sew Seam #4 on the center of the back, leaving open where marked.

3. Cut out. Sew the darts on both sides of the bottom of the back.

4. Place the front of the body on the fold, and then cut out. Pin the Body Front to the Body Back, right sides together.

5. Machine sew the body pieces all the way around, starting at the top of the neck.

6. Clip the curves, turn the pieces right side out, and fill the body firmly with stuffing. Place a pipe cleaner in the neck and pack stuffing firmly around the pipe cleaner. This prevents the head from drooping later.

7. Cut out the Breasts. Trace the darts and machine sew them, right sides together.

8. Place a small amount of stuffing in each Breast. Pin the Breasts to the chest.

9. With your fingers, turn under the edges of the Breasts and hand sew them to the chest with a ladder stitch (see Embroidery Stitches, page 108). Slip a little more stuffing inside each breast to fill them out. Close the Breasts, and set the body aside.

10. Machine sew the Legs all the way around, starting from the toes, leaving open where marked. Cut out the Legs with pinking shears.

11. Before turning, the toes must be sewn. Pin the toe section together with seams matching, as shown below. Draw in the type of feet you want, or use the guide in the illustration below.

12. Machine sew the toes along the line you drew. Clip the curves.

13. Cut slits at the top of each Leg, where marked. You will cut a slit only on one side. (See template, page 114.)

14. Fill the Legs with stuffing through the slits, and then use a whip stitch to close them. Set the Legs aside.

15. Machine sew the Arms all the way around, starting from the opening at the wrist, leaving open where marked.

16. Cut out the Arms, clip the curves, and turn them right side out. Fill with stuffing. Set the Arms aside.

17. Lower the stitch length on your sewing machine from 2.0 to 1.5.

18. Carefully machine sew around the Hands, leaving open where marked. When you get to the fingers, you must machine sew two stitches across each fingertip, and two stitches between each finger. Otherwise it will be almost impossible to turn the fingers.

[Steps 18–19]
Cut out hands after they are sewn

19. Cut out each Hand. Use your scissors to clip between each finger. Turn the Hands, using your favorite turning tools. Insert wires in the fingers, if you wish. Fill them with stuffing.

20. Hand sew the Hands to the Arms. Don't worry about the stitches; the wrist will be covered up later on. Set the Arms aside. They won't be attached until the dress is on the body.

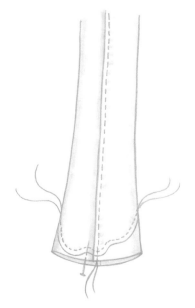

[Steps 11–12]
Illustration 3
Drawing and sewing toes

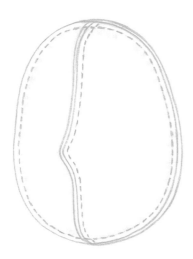

[Step 2]
Sew Face to Back of Head

The Head

1. Machine sew Seam #1 on the Face, and Seam #2 on the Back of Head, leaving open where marked.

2. Cut out the two pieces. Open up the Face and the Back of Head. Pin them, right sides together. Machine sew all the way around, leaving open where marked. Clip the curves, and turn right side out. Fill firmly with stuffing, and set aside. Don't worry about the stuffing in the nose. The sculpting will keep the stuffing in there.

3. Machine sew the Ears. Cut out the pieces, turn right side out, and top stitch by machine. To do this, draw in pencil the lines you want for the inside of the ear. Then sew by machine.

4. Attach the Ears to the head with needle and thread.

5. Hand sew the head to the neck of the body.

Gather your drawing and sculpting materials.

Drawing and Sculpting the Face

As with the flat face, you must first draw a grid. This time the grid is simpler, because there are already some reference points on the face from the sewing and stuffing.

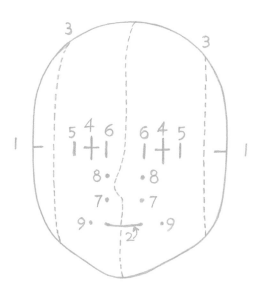

Simple grid for a profiled head

1. The seam designates the center of the face, lengthwise. To locate the center point widthwise, find where the nose starts to curve out, below the forehead. This is generally the center point between the forehead and the chin. When you have found this point, mark it with a pencil on either side of the center seam (#1).

2. Locate the halfway point between the nose and the chin. Make a mark here (#2).

3. To locate the center of the eyes, you must "slice" off a section on either side of the head. Look at the forehead to see where the top of the head starts to curve outward. Draw several dashes down the side of the head (#3).

4. Find the halfway point between one of these dashes and the center seam. Make a vertical pencil mark (#4) here; it should fall on the horizontal pencil mark (#1). Do the same on the other side.

5. For the width of each eye, you will halve each half. From each "slice" (#3) to #4, find the halfway point. Make a vertical pencil mark here (#5). Do the same on the other side.

6. Halfway between #4 and the center seam of the face, make a pencil mark (#6).

   You should have one eye width between each eye. The width and the height of the eye will be the same. Refer to Chapter 1 (page 14), for more detail on drawing eyes.

7. Measure the width of the eye, and make a pencil mark above and below #1. Draw a square, using the pencil marks as a reference.

8. The nostrils are next. You'll see a slight curve inward on the face. On each side of the center seam, directly down from #6 (the inside of the eye), make a small dot with the pencil (#7).

9. Each flare of the nose is straight up from the nostril, and halfway from the inside corner of the eye. Make a pencil mark on each side of the center seam for the flares (#8). Refer to the close-up illustration below for these two steps.

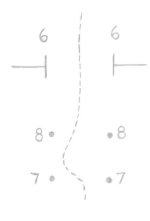

[Step 8–9]
Close-up of nose

10. The outside corners of the lips are directly below the #4 marker. Make a small dot with the pencil (#9), in line with the center of the mouth (#2).

[Step 11]
Drawing and outlining the face

11. Following the techniques in Chapter 1 (page 14), draw the eyeballs, irises, pupils, lips, and eyebrows. Outline these with a brown pen, and erase the unnecessary pencil marks. (See Chapter 2, page 24, for more about outlining.)

12. This face will not have eyelids completely drawn; separate ones will be added.

13. Thread the 3" (7.6 cm) sculpting needle with 1 yard (0.9 m) of strong thread, and tie a knot in the end. Anchor the thread to the back of her head (that is, take a stitch in the back of the head). If you do not anchor the thread in the back of the head, the knot could pop through the face. Refer to the chart on page 47 as you sculpt.

14. Push your needle into the head and out at #1 (the inside corner of the eye).

[Steps 15–16]
Sculpting the nose

15. Go back into the head, but not too close from where you came out. This can be a vertical or a horizontal stitch. Go down to the opposite nostril (#2). As you go in and out, pull your thread to define the features—but not too tightly, or you'll get wrinkles. This is also when you'll get the stuffing back in the nose. As you sew, use your needle to pull stuffing toward the face.

16. Go back into the head, up and over to the opposite flare (#3), back into the head, and straight across to the other flare (#4).

17. Go back into the head, down to the opposite nostril (#5), back into the head, and up to the opposite inside corner of the eye (#6).

18. Go back into the head, and down to the outside corner of the mouth (#7), on the same side of the face. Go back into the head, and up to the outside corner of the eye (#8).

19. Go back into the head, and over to the inside corner of the opposite eye (#1). Go back into the head, and down to the outside corner of the lips (#9). Go back into the head, and up to the outside corner of the eye (#10).

20. Go back into the head, and then to the back of the head. Anchor off.

[Step 17]
Stitching from nose to eye

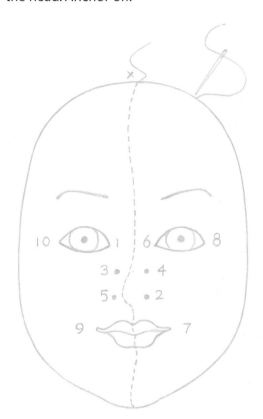

[Steps 13–20]
Chart of sculpting points

Coloring the Head

For this doll, you'll use colored pencils. There are many types and brands. All work fine on cloth, but the best are oil-based. These include Sanford Prismacolor (Karisma, internationally), Walnut Hollow Oil Pencils, and Van Gogh's Colored Pencils.

1. Start with the shading. Use sienna brown, if you have it, or another light brown. Shade the temples, around where the crease of the eyelids will be, down the sides of the nose, under the nose, around the flares, down the center seam under the nose, under the lower lip, and around the chin. Decide where your light is coming from, and shade a bit beyond the chin, toward the cheek on the shaded side of the face. Shade lightly on the upper lip, around the crease of the smile, and under the eyelids. Really rub in the color; when it is blended, it will fade quite a bit.

2. Next, with a lighter tan or beige pencil, add highlights. These are near the shading, but toward the higher points of the face: on the temples, down the sides of the nose, on the upper lip, on the chin, under the eyes, on the cheekbones, and below the eyebrows, on the brow bone.

3. Use a white pencil to lighten the center of the forehead, the tan or beige area under the eyes, the cheekbones, and the center of the chin. This may not show on your fabric, but it is very important. When the face is blended, you will see how the white prevents the other colors from covering an area.

4. Lastly, use carmine red on cheek area. Put it exactly where you would put blush on a human face, but really layer it on. (See the highlighting guide in Chapter 2, page 25. Also, refer to the photo below for these steps.)

5. Wrap a piece of fabric around your index finger, and use it to blend the colors. On the sample head (below), one side is blended, and the other side is not. This shows how dark to color with the pencils. As you can see, the colors blend beautifully.

6. The eyes are next. Use three shades of one color, or three different colors in varying shades (a light, a medium, and a dark). The sample eye uses light green, grass green, and peacock blue.

[Step 1–5]
Right side of face is blended

[Steps 6–11]
Left side of face is finished

7. With the lightest shade, fill in the iris. On the side of the iris that would be in the shadow, use the medium shade; color that side and underneath the eyelid. Use the darkest shade to trace an edge where the eyelid will be, darken the upper part of the iris, and touch the upper part of the pupil. (See Chapter 1, page 19, for a detailed illustration of the eyes.)

8. The lips are colored the same way as in the previous chapters. (See Chapter 1, page 19, for how to add life to the lips.)

9. When you have finished the face, seal it with a textile medium, and let dry for 24 hours. It is best to do this before detailing the face, or the pens can pick up the pigment from the pencils, and get clogged.

10. While the face is drying, start on the eyelids. Cut out the eyelids. Use the end of a toothpick to put a thin band of glue along the lower edge of each eyelid. Place three false eyelashes along the outer edge of each eyelid, angling them to make sure you have a right eye and a left eye. Let dry.

11. Once the face is dry, use a black pen to fill in the pupil.

12. Use a white gel pen, or white paint and a small brush, to add a dot of highlight to each pupil, on the side of the eye that catches the light. (This is an important part of doing a face. The eyes are the windows to the soul; without this highlight, the eyes are dead.) Use your white pen or paint to whiten the whites of the eyes.

13. Add a dot of red to the inside of each eye for the tear duct (refer to Chapter 1, page 19, for details).

14. Use a contrasting-colored pen to outline the iris, and draw the rods that radiate from the pupil.

15. Use a toothpick to spread a bit of glue along the upper edge of each eyelid. Place the eyelids over the eyes. Press them down, and lift up the center of the eyelids; this will make them look more natural. Let dry. The sample head (below) has just one eyelid, so that you can see the difference.

16. Add eyeliner with a black or brown pen.

17. To color the eyelids, start with colored pencils. The inside of the sample eyelid is colored with Process Red, and the outside with Mediterranean Blue. Next, blend the colors with a small blending stick, such as Tsukineko's Fantastix. Finally, apply glitter gel pens in matching colors.

18. Add some yellow to the upper part of the eyelid and up toward the brow. Use purple in the eye crease and down each side of the nose. On top of this, use glitter gel pens.

19. To hide the crease where the eyelid was glued, use metallic fabric paint, such as Lumiere or Stewart Gill's Byzantia paints.

20. Seal the face with the textile medium.

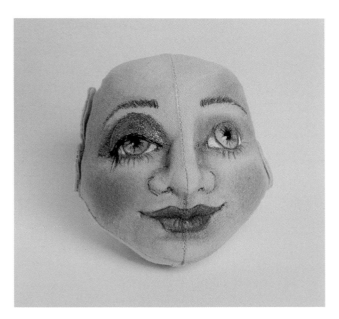

[Steps 15–19]
Add eyelids to eyes

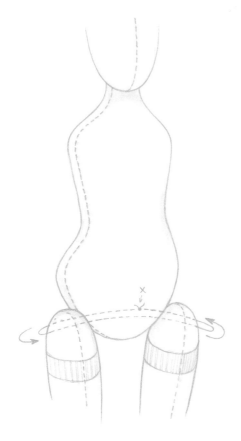

[Step 2]
Create stockings

[Step 9]
Attach legs to body

Stockings and Shoes

It is easier to make the stockings and shoes before the legs are attached to the body.

1. Take one stocking from a pair of knee-hi's, and turn it wrong side out.

2. Machine sew, using a stretch stitch, from the bottom of the stocking up to the top, on one side. Do the same on the other side. This will create two doll stockings. Cut out the stockings, turn them right side out, and slip them on the legs. (See illustration, left.)

3. Trace two Shoe Soles on the wrong side of the fabric you have chosen for the shoes.

4. Cut a slit down the center of each traced Shoe Sole.

5. Double the fabric, right sides together, and sew all the way around. Cut out the Shoe Soles, and turn them right side out through the slit.

6. Cut out two Inner Soles from the piece of felt. Slip one into each Shoe Sole. Set aside.

7. Cut three ribbons, each 1 yard (0.9 m) long, for each Shoe.

8. Wrap three ribbons around each foot, criss-crossing from front to back. Tie the ribbons in an overhand knot at the front of the foot, just above the ankle. Hand sew beads at the center of the ribbons, as shown (right). (Instructions for making the beaded flowers are on pages 81–82.) Hand sew the soles to the bottom of the feet.

9. Hand sew the Legs to the sides of the Body, as shown (left), using a long sculpting needle and strong thread.

The Dress

1. Cut the four different layers of the skirt.
   a. Bottom layer: 20" (51 cm) wide by 10" (25 cm) long
   b. Third layer: 20" (51 cm) wide by 8½" (22 cm) long
   c. Second layer: 20" (51 cm) wide by 7½" (19 cm) long
   d. Top layer: 18" (46 cm) wide by 6½" (16 cm) long

2. Seal the edges of the fabric with a candle by running the edge of the silk along the edge of the flame to slightly melt it. Because silk can flare up, put your candle in a pie plate that has a little water in the bottom.

3. Machine sew the back seams of each layer, one by one, right sides together.

4. Put the layers in order, with the bottom layer first. Machine gather all layers together at the waist. It is best to use a quilting thread for this. That way, when you pull the threads to gather the skirt, the thread won't break.

5. Slip the layered skirt on the doll. Pull the threads to fit the waist, and hand sew with needle and thread directly to the body, using a running stitch.

6. Wrap the bridal lace around the doll to measure for the bodice. Cut the lace to fit, leaving enough at the back to overlap a bit.

7. Cut out the motif at the bottom of the bodice. Use any shape you like. The sample doll's bodice is staggered, giving interest to the dress.

8. Hand sew the bodice directly to the body. It is best to do this with a beading needle and thread. Some of the beads may be loose from the cutting of the lace. As you tack the lace to the body, use your needle and thread to secure any loose beads.

9. The sleeves are also made from bridal lace. Cut pieces to fit from the wrists up to the biceps, or just above the elbows. Hand sew in place, again catching any loose beads. Note: This is done before the arms are attached to the body.

10. With one of the same fabrics used in the skirt, cut out the sleeves. The sleeves are two pieces of fabric, each measuring 6½" x 5" (16.5 x 12.7 cm).

11. With right sides together, machine sew up the back seam. Turn sleeves right side out, and slip them onto the arms.

12. Bunch up the sleeves, and hand sew them in place with a beading needle and thread. Sew on matching beads as desired.

13. Hand sew the arms in place, using strong thread and a hand sewing needle. Anchor the thread at the shoulders, then go into the arm. Sew through the sleeve fabric as you go into the arm. You won't go all the way through the arm, just partway, then back into the shoulder. Repeat at least three times, then anchor off on the body, under the arm. Do the same with the other arm.

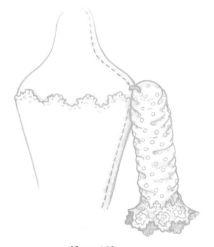

[Step 13]
Hand sew arms to shoulders

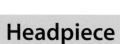

Headpiece

1. Cut one 7" (18 cm) square from each of three silk fabrics used for the skirt.

2. Fold two of the squares into two triangles. Roll each triangle into a long shape, starting with the narrow end, rolling toward the longer edge.

3. Wrap one of these long pieces around her head, and hand sew in place.

4. Place the second long piece under the first one, making sure it shows. Hand sew in place.

5. Gather the last square at its center and place it inside the first two. Hand sew in place.

6. Cut five of the ribbons into 7" (18 cm) lengths. Cut three silk ribbons into 7" (18 cm) lengths.

7. Tie all of the ribbons together at the center. Hand sew them to the center of the doll's head.

Add some pearls to her neck, pin a brooch to her headpiece, and she's finished!

Chrysalis, Empress of Butterflies

JUDY SKEEL

The artist writes:

I began the face for Chrysalis, Empress of Butterflies, knowing she would be a fantasy creature with elfin ears, large innocent eyes, and coloring based on her costume. Because the face needed to be sculpted, I made a seam down the center so that I could sculpt her nose, eyes, lips, and chin.

Before sculpting the face, I lightly drew the features with a terra-cotta Prismacolor pencil. Once the features were drawn, I traced them with a Micron 0.005 brown pen. The eyes are colored with gel pens: white for the whites of the eyes, black for the pupil, and for the iris, a combination of lavender and purple, with fine lines of blue for the rods. A final touch of white paint creates the "spark of life" dot on the right side of each iris.

For Chrysalis, I used a light application of fuchsia Prismacolor pencil for blush, and layered it on top of the burgundy gel pen on her lips. The gel pen gives a solid base color, while the pencils give a wider palette for her makeup. Fuchsia is also used for eye makeup on the inner corners of the eyes, tying all the features together with a common color.

While keeping upper and lower eye shadow lighter than above the crease in the eyelid, I chose to use metallic blue and purple Prismacolor pencils to blend to the fuchsia in the inner corners of the eyes. Going back to the white gel pen, I added a stroke of white just under the creases in the eyelids. This really makes the eyelids pop out. A small splash of white on the lips, on the same side as the sparks of light in the eyes, gives a rounded appearance and allows them to look wet.

Chrysalis's fantasy eyes required long, luxurious lashes, so for a final touch I used a black brush tip Micron pen for the top lashes, and 0.005 brown and black pens for the lower lashes and the brows. The face was heat set, and then sealed with two layers of Workable Fixatif and a final coat of Craftguard.

Forget-Me-Not Fairy

KAREN SMITH

The artist writes:

Alaska's summers, in which the longest day is more than nineteen hours long, allow my favorite flower, the forget-me-not, to grow in my garden. This is also our state flower. When Patti asked me to make a doll for her book, I knew I had to incorporate this flower into my doll.

My favorite fabric to use for sculpting is Pimatex cotton. I fill my dolls' faces very firmly, and this cotton holds up very well during the sculpting. Before sculpting, I lightly drew in the features with a mechanical pencil, and then outlined them with a brown Micron pen. Following Patti's basic sculpting techniques, I sculpted the eyes, nose, and lips.

Because I wanted the doll to be softly colored, I used a combination of Prismacolor pencils and Micron pens. Sienna brown was used for the shading, along with Peach. The lips were colored with Magenta and Scarlet Lake. The eyes were a combination of Olive Green and Periwinkle. For the blush on her cheeks, I used my own "people" blush.

When I had completed the doll head that captured what I had envisioned, I looked out my window just beyond my sewing table, and watched the setting sun. It was 11:30 pm!

Lady Juliana at Ascot

SHAWN ASIALA

The artist writes:

I had such a good time making this doll! I modified the original pattern by reducing it 25 percent and making the legs straight, enabling the doll to stand and show off her dress. She has a wire armature body, so she's able to stand on her own. I wanted her to be very curvaceous, so I added shapely hips and a bosom. The face was made with pima cotton and is lightly sculpted. I used Prismacolor pencils to shade and color the face. Zig pens were used to outline and accentuate details. The white highlights were applied with gel roller pens. I incorporated "real" eyelashes with the eyeliner, and glued them on the eyelids. A bead in each iris added sparkle to the face. The hair is sewn on the head, and then "styled" with a wool felting needle.

Juliana's hat is made from a ladies' wool hat. I cut out the top part of the hat, and sewed a sturdy wire into the edge, enabling me to shape it. I sewed the hat on the head, and then I added the ribbons, flowers, and feathers.

Her bodice is created from pieces of lace that are sewn on to create a fitted look. Her skirt is an empire design, gathered at the bodice, with a short bustled train in the back.

Minn and her Muse, Saar

HEATHER COOPER

The artist writes:

My initial idea was to create a romantic, pretty woodland crea-ture, but to no avail. My heart belongs to the gypsy and ethnic looks, so out came the wonderful bag of very bright fabrics, braids, and embellishments bought for me in the bazaars of Pakistan by a friend of my mother.

Silk is one of my favorite fabrics to work with. I dyed the silk body fabric in shades of sienna, yellow green, and red. I used the Advanced Head along with the second body pattern, but straightened the legs. Using Patti's face-sculpting techniques, I drew the features with a pencil, and then sculpted with needle and thread. The facial features were embroidered using two strands of cotton. I used a combination of satin and herring-bone stitch. The embroidery was carried back into the hairline with overlapping layers of herringbone stitch, as well as some couched layers of frayed fabric and textured thread and braid.

Iris folding cards formed the idea for the structure of the bodice, and then the herringbone stitch used on the bodice was carried down from the face. Because the head looked over-whelmed by the strong colors of the costume, I sewed buttons and charms around the head to add width and texture.

The use of buttons was carried through to Saar, the peacock, to provide an integrated look.

Primavera

LALY TAPIA

The artist writes:

As I sat down with Patti's pattern, I began to think about the doll's face and the colors of fabric I would use for the body, arms, and legs. I decided to use green fabric that would make the body look like the stem of a flower. I used a sheer fabric to make a short skirt of "leaves." But the most important part, for me, was to make the face special for Patti's book.

I started hand-sculpting the face with very tiny stitches, beginning with the nose, and going from one side to the other until I reached the area where the nostrils begin. Using a clockwise system, from one side to the other, I made her nostrils. The lips were sculpted with very small stitches. I drew her eyes with an air-soluble pencil, and started making tiny stitches from the front of the face to the back (back and forth). When I finished the eyes, I painted them with acrylic paints and gel pens. To make her cheeks round, I made some stitches going from the eyes to the mouth. As I did this, I used my needle to lift a little bit of the stuffing.

To make the "petals" of her face, I cut some fancy sheer material in a bright yellow color. I made her "stem" with some velvet fabric. I turned it and rolled it through her body, so that it came out like a hat at the back of her head.

Working with Paint

2 4

Painting a face is one way of creating a unique doll. There are many fabric paints on the market that give a soft feel to the face, as well as many techniques. One is to cover the face of the doll with gesso, and then use acrylic or oil paints. In this chapter, I'll use two techniques. The contributing artists use a few additional paints and techniques. This will give you many ideas for creating fun and unique faces.

Magdalene

Head pattern #3 (pages 116–117) is used on this doll to give a more adult look. Fabric paints are used to add dimension to the face. These give more vibrancy as well. Body pattern #2 (pages 112–113) is used, but with changes to a leg and an arm, and some tucks added in the body. These change the positioning of the doll. Using simple tucks here and there on any cloth doll body can add excitement to its body attitude.

Materials

1/2 yard (46 cm) white cotton for the body

thread to match

6 pipe cleaners for the fingers

good-quality stuffing

1/4 yard (23 cm) batik cotton for the bodice and shoes

1/4 yard (23 cm) polyester fabric for the skirt

5 yards (4.6 m) each of 3 different yarns for embellishments

rayon and metallic sewing machine thread

mohair for hair

scraps of organza in 3 colors for embellishments

water-soluble stabilizer (Mokuba's Free Lace is an excellent choice)

5 colors of seed beads, size 11

five 6-mm Miracle beads

one hundred 4-mm crystals

beading thread and needles

1' (30 cm) 24-gauge beading wire

fabric paints (Jacquard's Textile and Lumiere, or Stewart Gill's Byzantia and Alchemy, are good choices)

Jacquard's Dye-Na-Flow in yellow, white, and red

Portfolio Series Water Soluble Oil Pastels

Tsukineko's Fantastix (optional)

Krylon's Workable Fixative, or other aerosol workable fixative

gesso

acrylic paints

paint brushes in various sizes, including small detail brushes

strong thread for sculpting

rubber stamps

Zig Millennium or Micron Pigma pens in black, red, and brown

gel pens in white, red, and a color for the eyes

various colored markers for acrylic face (colors to outline eyes, eyelashes, lips, and any additional detailing)

Tools

stuffing and turning tools

hand sewing needles

free-motion or darning foot for your sewing machine

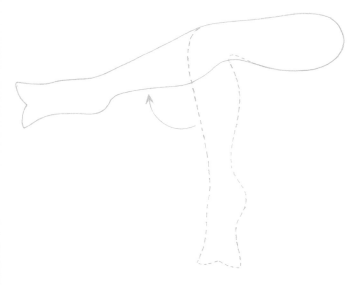

[Step 2]
Drawing a bent leg from the pattern

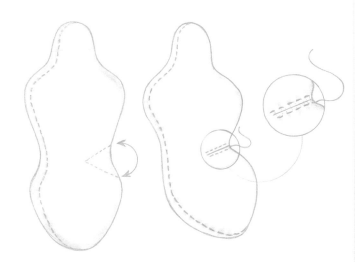

[Step 3]
Adding curves to the body with ladder stitches

Body Construction

1. Following the instructions for Body pattern #2 in Chapter 3 (page 42), sew everything but the head. This project uses Head pattern #3 (pages 116–117).

2. You will note that one leg is straight. I simply redrew one leg by tracing the upper leg, and then shifted the pattern to trace the lower leg (left).

3. After the body is filled with stuffing, sew a ladder stitch on one side of the waist to give it the curve needed so she'll rest on the other side (below, left).

4. Repeat the procedure from step 3 at the inside of the elbow to bend one arm.

The Head

1. Trace the two headpieces onto the wrong side of the fabric, making sure the arrow is on the grain line.

2. Sew Seam #1 on the Face, and Seam #2 on the Head Back. Back stitch at chin and bottom of back of head.

3. Cut out both pieces. Turn the back of the head right side out, and slip it into the Face. Pin them together, right sides together (right).

4. Sew from the top of the head down to the x. Back stitch here.

5. Sew the other side from the top of the head down to the other x.

6. Clip the curves, and turn the Head right side out. Fill it firmly with stuffing. This head can look very narrow if you don't fill out the jaw line and the cheeks.

   Push the stuffing into these areas. You'll be amazed at the amount of stuffing you can pack in.

7. Hand sew the Head to the Neck, using a ladder stitch.

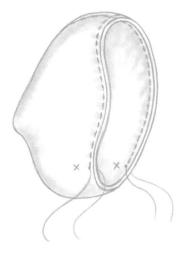

[Steps 3–5]
Sew Head Back to Face, right sides together

[Step 6]
The left head does not have enough stuffing in the cheeks and jaw
The right head is filled correctly

Drawing and Sculpting the Head

1. Follow the instructions in Chapter 3 (page 45), for both the drawing and sculpting of this head. Even though it is slightly different in shape, it is drawn and sculpted in the same manner.

2. After the face is drawn and sculpted, outline the features with a brown fabric pen.

Painting the Head

Fabric paints were used for the sample doll. The following are formulas that I used to mix the flesh and shading colors.

Flesh formula:

Jacquard's Textile, Lumiere, and Dye-Na-Flow Paints

Textile Paints:

1 part Russet

1 part Goldenrod

4 parts White

Mixed with:

2 parts Lumiere Pearl White

1 part Dye-Na-Flow Golden Yellow

Add 2 parts water.

1. Paint all flesh parts with this formula.

2. For shading, use 2 parts flesh formula mixed with ½ part Russet Textile Paint and ¼ part Violet Dye-Na-Flow. You could mix with brown, but I find these colors warmer and more realistic.

3. Shade down the sides of the nose, around the upper crease of the eyelid, under the nose and around the flare of the nose, under the lower lip, and along the temples. Refer to the photos on pages 25 and 26 as you shade the head.

4. Using 1 part White Textile Paint mixed with 1 part Pearl White Lumiere, add highlights to the forehead, down the center of the nose, on both flares of the nose, on the center of the chin, on the cheekbones, and on the brow. Refer to the photo for placement of the highlights.

[Step 6]
Fill in eyes with white paint

5. For the cheeks, put a small amount of the flesh formula in a container, and add Magenta. Load up a brush with this color, and dab quite a bit of it onto a piece of paper towel. Blush her cheeks with this brush.

AUTHOR'S SUGGESTION

The technique described in Step 5 is called dry brushing. It gives you more control with the paint.

6. Use the white paint to fill in the entire eye area.

7. Magdalene's irises are next. They are two shades of blue: a light blue and a medium blue. Fill in the irises with the light blue (or the light color you want to use). You'll use a small brush for this. With the medium color, darken the side of each iris that is in the shadow.

8. The eye shadow on the sample doll is a metallic blue with pewter added. With a small brush, color around the upper crease of the eye, and a bit under the eyelid. This gives a vampish look.

9. While the eye shadow is drying, color the lips. Again, use two shades: a medium and dark red, rose, or other color of your choice. Fill in the lips with the medium color. Next, use the darker color on the upper lip and the side of the lips that are in shadow. Let her lips dry.

10. When the eyes are dry, use a small brush and black paint to add the pupil.

11. Add a dot of red to the inside corner of each eye.

Close-up of finished face

12. Color the rest of the body with the paints of your choice. Magdalene has a red upper body and arms, and yellow legs.

13. After the body is dry, use rubber stamps and Lumiere paint to stamp her body.

14. After the body is stamped, let it dry for 24 hours, then heat set. There are several choices for heat setting. Place the doll on a sweater rack, in a clothes dryer set on the cotton setting for 30 minutes, or in an oven set at 225˚F (105˚C) for 15 minutes. Whatever you do, don't microwave her. There's enough wire in her wrists to cause her to fry. Plus, it wouldn't be good for your microwave.

15. When the doll is dry, it is time to do the detail work. Start by outlining the eyelids with a black Zig or Micron pen. Use this same pen to draw thin eyebrows. With a white gel pen, add a dot of white to each pupil.

16. Dot the nostrils with a brown pen, and draw the flare on each side of her nose.

17. Use a red pen to outline the upper and lower lips, and draw the creases. For the center of the mouth, use a brown pen. A red pen just doesn't show up.

18. Using a contrasting gel pen, outline the irises and draw in the rods that radiate out from the pupil. Use the black Zig or Micron pen to draw in the eyelashes.

AUTHOR'S SUGGESTION

When using Lumiere on rubber stamps, have some water and an old toothbrush nearby. Lumiere, or any metallic or pearlized paints, will dry quickly on the stamps, clogging them up. As soon as you are finished stamping, clean the stamps with water and the toothbrush.

Using Acrylic Paints

Acrylic paints are a bit different from fabric paints. Actually, most fabric paints are simply acrylic paints with a textile medium added. This allows the fabric to be painted without the paint making the fabric stiff. In painting a cloth doll head with acrylic paints, you get an entirely different look.

When painting with acrylics, you have to work quickly. They dry almost immediately. You can add products called extenders to the paint to slow the drying time. Golden has one called Acrylic Glazing Liquid that gives you approximately 45 minutes to work on the face before the paints dry.

1. Start with a head that has been filled with stuffing, and cover it with gesso. Allow it to dry, and then sand it with fine sandpaper.

2. Do this two more times. It takes about three coats of gesso to seal the head.

3. Once the last coat of gesso is dry (this generally takes about one hour), paint the head with the paints of your choice.

I find working with acrylics most appropriate for creating a whimsical or fantasy doll.

AUTHOR'S SUGGESTION

Kandy Scott made some unique faces using the gesso and acrylic paint technique. For the detail work on her Mardi Gras lady, she used markers called Painters. After everything was dry, she sprayed the face with a gloss fixative.

Artist Arley Berryhill (see Gallery, page 83) used acrylic paints to add texure to Lady in Red's expressive face

Artist Li Hertzi (see Gallery, page 105) used acrylic paints over the entire body of Wide Open to show off her bright, energized posture

[Steps 1–7]
Color face with oil pastels

[Step 14]
Detail of oil pastel–drawn face

Using Oil Pastels

Oil pastels are probably my favorite painting medium. I use these in my paper journaling, and have found them equally exciting to use on fabric.

1. Start with a finished fabric head, and color the entire head with peach pastel.

2. Next, following the chart in Chapter 3 (page 25), color in the shadows with a combination of golden brown, medium brown, and violet.

3. Highlight the high points of the face with white.

4. Using pink and red-orange, color in the cheeks.

5. Fill in the eye area with white. Add a bit of the blue for the irises.

6. Color in the lips with red-orange.

7. Add some yellow to the outer part of the eyelids.

8. Using a dampened stencil brush, or Tsukineko's Fantastix, blend these colors.

9. Deepen the crease of the eyelids with more violet and blue-violet. With True Blue, lighten the sides of the irises that would catch the light. Deepen the upper part of the irises with blue-violet.

10. Continue blending as you go along.

11. Add more highlights to the forehead, the center of the nose, and the chin.

12. Darken the center of the lips and the upper lip with red.

13. Spray the face with Krylon's Workable Fixative, or another fixing solution.

14. Add detail work, following techniques described for the other faces.

[Step 5]
Zigzag yarns to seams of bustier

Creating Clothing

1. Cut two each of the Bustier pieces (pages 116–118).

2. Pin the Center Front Seam #1 to the Side Front Seam #2, wrong sides together. Zigzag stitch these by machine, from the top to the bottom. Do the same with the other side.

3. Pin the Back piece together at Seam #4, wrong sides together, and sew from the top to the bottom.

4. Pin the Front Bustier to the Back at Seam #3. Zigzag stitch by machine, wrong sides together.

5. Using one of your yarns, zigzag stitch the yarn to both sides of the seam by machine.

6. With right sides together, sew the shoulder seam, joining Seam #5 to Seam #6.

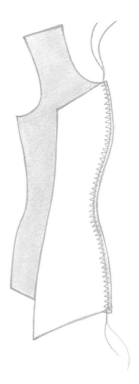

[Step 2]
Sew Center Front to Side Front using a zigzag stitch

Skirt detail

AUTHOR'S SUGGESTION

If you can get Mokuba's Free Lace stabilizer, use this. It has one sticky side that holds the circles. You then place the clear sheet on top, and it adheres to the sticky piece. It makes life so easy.

7. Machine sew the yarn along the upper edge of the bustier all the way around, starting on the left side front. When you reach the right side front, zigzag down the front.

8. Machine sew more yarn to the arm openings, as described above.

9. The bottom of the bustier is left unhemmed. This will be covered up with the embellishments.

10. The skirt is 20" (51 cm) wide by 8½" (22 cm) long. Machine sew the back seam, right sides together.

11. Turn under a hem ⅛" (3 mm) wide. Zigzag stitch in place. Edge the hem with yarn by machine sewing the yarn in place.

12. Machine sew a running stitch along the waist, and pull to gather. Slip the skirt onto the body, and hand sew it in place, just below the waist.

13. Slip the bustier onto the body, and adjust to fit at the center front. Pin it in place.

14. Sew crystals down the front of the bodice to close it, and to give the look of sparkling buttons. Mark the bodice so that the crystals are ⅜" (1 cm) apart.

15. To make the ruffles that create the edge of the bustier, cut 11 circles from each of the 3 pieces of organza. You'll have 33 circles.

16. Place these, one by one, between two sheets of water-soluble stabilizer. Pin in place.

17. With the rayon thread in the upper threader of your machine, and the metallic thread in your bobbin, free-motion machine sew lacy edges around each of the circles. (See photo, page 77.)

[Steps 16–18]
Free-motion machine sew on circles of fabric

18. In free-motion machine work, the key is to create a base of threads for the top machine threadwork to lock onto. It is important to make sure that, as you sew, your threads connect with each other. Start on the circle of fabric, and then run along the edge. The samples were sewn with circular machining around the edges. This circular sewing was done several times, going around and around along the edge of the fabric.

19. Dissolve the stabilizer according to the manufacturer's recommendation. Let the circles dry.

20. When they are dry, place three circles on top of each other, alternating the colors.

21. Sew them together at the center in a circle. Pull the thread to gather them, and then hand sew them along the edge of the bustier. At the center front, sew a beaded flower. The instructions for the flower are at the end of this chapter (page 81).

22. Cut three different yarns into 10" (25 cm) lengths. You'll need enough of these to put one between each of the ruffles. Tie the yarn bundles at the center, and then hand sew them between the ruffles.

23. At the shoulders, tie the bundles into a bow, and hand sew along the edge of the bustier.

24. Cover the wrist area with beads or trim to hide the seams.

[Steps 7–8]
Hand sew a beaded flower at center of Shoe Top

The Shoes

1. Cut out four Shoe Soles from the same fabric. Set aside.

2. Trace two Shoe Tops on the wrong side of the fabric. Double the fabric, right sides together, and sew along Seam #1. Cut out both Shoe Tops. Turn, right side out.

3. Cut a slit down the center of one of the Shoe Soles. You'll do this for both shoes.

4. Pin the Shoe Tops to the Shoe Soles that aren't slit, right sides together. On top of these, pin the Soles that have been slit.

5. Sew all the way around the outer edge of the shoe along Seam #2.

6. Turn the shoes through the slits, and push out the sides of the shoes.

7. Place the shoes over the feet of your doll. Hand sew three of the yarns, cut in 24" (61 cm) lengths, along each of the Shoe Tops. Start attaching them at the center of the shoe, and at the center of the yarn. Follow the upper edge of the Shoe Tops. As you hand sew the yarns, they will go through the foot, too. This secures the shoes to the feet.

8. When you get to the sides, wrap the rest of the yarns around the legs, and tie them in a bow about mid-shin. With a needle and thread, tack the yarns to the legs.

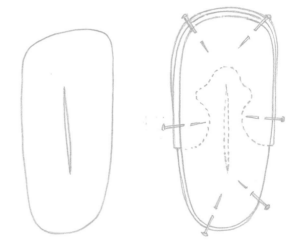

[Steps 3–4]
Cut a slit in one Shoe Sole and pin to remaining shoe parts

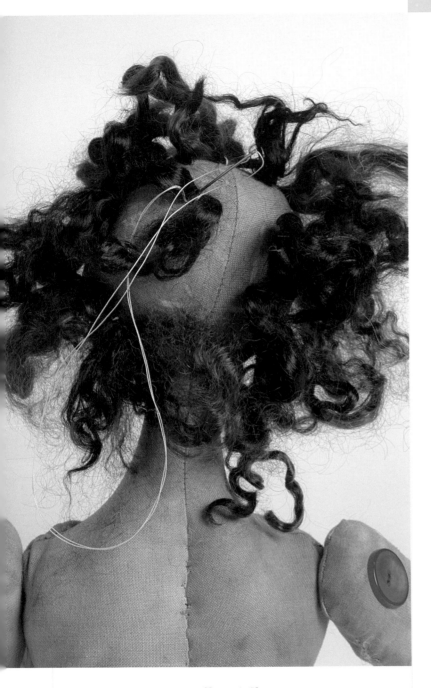

[Steps 1–3]
Hand sew mohair to head

Finishing

1. Hand sew mohair to the head, starting at the back of the head, and following the seam around.

2. Catch the mohair at its center with the needle and thread.

3. Once you have enough sections of mohair around the seams, fill in at the back of the head. Use your fingers to fluff up the mohair, and then pull it up, toward the top of the head, and secure it with needle and thread. Pull some strands out with a needle.

4. Sew a beaded flower to the hair, near where an ear would be.

Beaded Flowers

These beautiful flowers can be used on dolls, garments, quilts, jewelry, and any number of creations. If you are familiar with peyote beadwork, you'll find them very simple to make. If you aren't familiar with peyote beadwork, you'll still enjoy the process.

1. Assemble your supplies: Miracle or Wonder Beads, size 11 seed beads, beading thread, and needles.

2. Thread a beading needle with 2 yards (1.8 m) of beading thread. Don't tie a knot at the end of the thread.

3. Needle up enough size 11 seed beads to wrap around the Miracle Bead. You'll measure around the bead for now. Take the beads down towards the tail and tie them in a circle, using an overhand knot.

4. You'll now start doing a circular peyote stitch. Place one seed bead on the needle.

5. Skip the bead that is next to the bead that the thread has passed through, and go through the next bead.

6. Add another bead, skip a bead, and go through another bead. Continue this around the circle.

[Step 3]
String beads to wrap around Miracle Bead

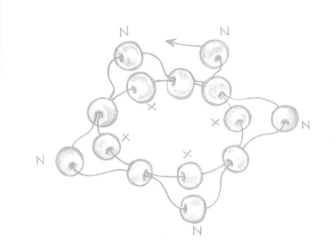

[Steps 4–6]
Circular peyote stitch

AUTHOR'S SUGGESTION

If you have an even number of beads on your circle, you'll need to do what is called a "step up" in peyote beadwork. This means that when you come out of your last bead in the circle, there won't be room to add another bead. You will go through the bead that is sticking up; it's called an "up" bead.

If you have an odd number of beads in your circle, you'll be able to add a bead, and then go through the "up" bead.

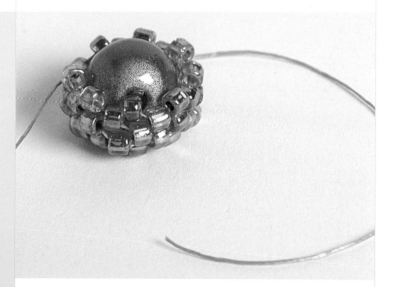

[Steps 6–8]
Creating rows of peyote beading, before stringing Miracle Bead

7. Continue around the circle three more times. After the third row, pull your beads and the beads will pull up into a cup.

8. After you have made four rows (the base row and the first row of peyote are considered Row #1), it is time to thread the Miracle Bead.

9. Weave down to a center bead in a three-bead stack.

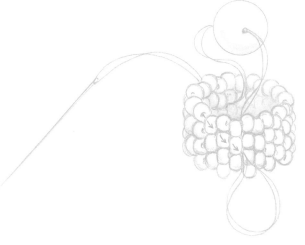

[Steps 9–11]
Add the Miracle Bead at the center of the peyote "cup"

10. Go to the inside of the cup, and pick up the Miracle Bead with the needle. Go straight across to the other side, and through a middle bead.

11. Go back inside and through the Miracle Bead, and over to the original side. Go into a seed bead, and then weave up to an "up" bead along the top edge.

12. Come out the "up" bead, and pick up four seed beads, one crystal, and one seed bead.

13. Skip the last seed bead, and go through the crystal and the #4 seed bead.

14. Pick up three more seed beads, and go over to the next "up" bead.

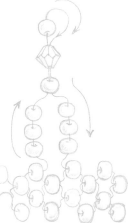

[Steps 12–14]
Create the beaded petals with seed beads and crystals

15. Continue doing this around the top of the cup.

16. For the next series of "petals," change colors of seed beads and crystals. With your needle, weave down to the next "down" bead. This will be between the petals you just made from one "up" bead to another. You'll now go from "down" bead to "down" bead.

17. Make another row of petals in the same manner. When you are finished, weave the needle down to the bottom, and attach the flower to the shoes, bodice, hair, or wherever.

The Lady in Red

ARLEY BERRYHILL

The artist writes:

This character is inspired by the great divas from the silent-movie era: Clara Bow, Theda Bara, Louise Brooks, and Gloria Swanson.

Using Patti's intermediate body pattern and the advanced head pattern, I first enlarged the head 10 percent. The mouth was needle sculpted, and extra dimension was added with thick acrylic paint.

The eyes are plastic shank buttons, painted with acrylics. Glitter glue was added to the irises for sparkle. A clear gloss was painted over the entire eye. The eyelids were applied over the buttons, and the eyelashes were glued on.

The hair is made of hackle feathers, which are individually glued on. The cigarette and holder are carved and sculpted from a wooden dowel.

Enigma

ROBYN TREFRY

The artist writes:

When I saw the pattern, it brought to mind the possibility of different faces being interchangeable. This evolved into the finished project.

The colors I chose to paint these doll faces came from the piece of fabric that was used for the doll's body. I find inspiration for faces in many places—makeup advertisements, drawings, comics, sculptures, and all types of art. I like to use acrylic paints with a 000 brush.

The idea for the white face stemmed from looking through a comics catalogue, which has inspiring artwork for faces, hair, and costuming. The eye color is the same as the natural face. The eyelids are done in blue metallic.

The more natural face uses browns with bronze metallic highlights around the eyes. I like to bring a little of the eyelid color around the outside of the eyes, and a little bit under the bottom lid to about halfway.

Each face gives the doll a different personality, and she may have more to come.

Puttin' on the Glitz

JACQUIE LECUYER

The artist writes:

My dolls tend to be inspired by the entertainment industry — the dancer, the actress, the glam queen, Cirque du Soleil, and others. Thus, my over-the-top face painting.

After the doll was made, I outlined the eyes, brows, and mouth with a brown waterproof pen. After the face was painted, I filled in the eye area with white paint. The cheeks were next, and I let the color leach out to give a nice blended effect. I used the cheek color on the eyelid to unify the face with similar tones.

Acrylic paints were used on the lips and the irises of the eyes. With a very fine brush, I applied eyeliner, lashes, brows, and lip liner. I finished the lips with black, as I find this balances the dark color of the eyes.

To seal the face I used Grumbacher's Final Fixative. Lastly, I used a sparkle glaze on the lips, eyelids, and cheeks.

Voilà, the Glitz!

Falon

ALLISON MARANO

The artist writes:

Creating Falon was a welcome challenge, because I don't normally use paint for a doll's face. However, I found that I could approach the design in the same way I do when using pencils and pens.

I began with a firmly stuffed head of white Pimatex cotton. Basic facial features were marked using an air-erase marker. Then the eyes, nose, and mouth were lightly sculpted, using a thin needle and white silk thread.

I created a basic light flesh tone with acrylic tube paints—titanium white, with small amounts of cadmium red light and yellow oxide added. This was then mixed with watered-down Createx fabric medium, and applied to the entire head with a flat synthetic brush.

Using the sculpted points as a guide, I drew the eyes and mouth on the painted face with a mechanical pencil. I drew the basic eye shapes on my dominant side first, and then flipped the head upside down to draw in the other eye. This made it easier to match my weak side.

For shading the recessed areas around the nose and above the eyelids, burnt sienna and raw umber were mixed with the basic flesh tone. For tints and highlights, I added more white. For the cheeks, I blended scarlet lake with the original flesh tone. The eye details and the lips were a mixture of various acrylic colors, some undiluted. Pure white was reserved for the eye highlights. Eyebrows and lashes were dotted in with Pigma pens.

After the face was dry, I gave it a light spray of final fixative in matte finish.

Miralys the Halibut Queen

JUDI WELLNITZ

The artist writes:

Miralys is holding her breath—she's not used to being a fish out of water! You can usually find her swimming with the halibut near the bottom of the ocean. She agreed to come up for air so we could discuss her fair features. Miralys began as Kaufman Pimatex cotton. Her nose, eyes, and mouth are sculpted using hand quilting thread, which is strong, yet not as thick, as button or upholstery thread. Minimal sculpting was done on the mouth and eyes. The mouth was drawn up to form a pleasant smile and to give some definition to the cheeks.

Her face and body are painted with a Stewart Gill brand pink pearlescent paint. I put her in the oven to heat set the paint. I used a .005 brown Pigma pen to draw the outlines of the eyes and mouth, and to define the nostrils and nose flares. The shading was completed using Caran d'Ache Prismalo watercolor pencils. I used Patti's basic shading instructions (see page 17) and then added some purple alongside the nose and above the eyelids. The eyes themselves are colored following Patti's face instructions. I also like to put a white highlight bisecting the eyelid. It really brightens the eyes. But there's no thrill like the one you get when you paint the white "eyelights" on the pupil—I used a white gel pen for that. The doll really comes alive and speaks to you then. The lips are colored with watercolor pencils and the lip lines are drawn with a .005 Pigma pen.

For her outfit: My doll club had a scarf dyeing party one day and I put a white T-shirt under my scarf for a second generation-dyed fabric. That T-shirt turned into her tail fabric. I shaped her tail with side fins, just like the halibut she hangs out with. Patti had taught me how to make free-motion embroidery lace, so I used that for her bra top, sleeves, and the netting on her tail.

Kidjo

IRENE PICHARD

The artist writes:

Kidjo is a young African woman who is wearing her most beautiful dress to go to a dance.

Being a new doll maker, I came up with a clever way to make things less stressful in drawing features:

1. Start by tracing the eyes with a pencil, and then filling in with white acrylic paint. When this is dry, sew a four-hole button in the middle of the white. The button now becomes the iris.

2. Sew four little beads into each hole, and one in the middle of the first four to form the pupil. Paint one or two little white dots on the little beads to give the eyes life.

3. Trace and cut out the eyelids, and glue false eyelashes along the lower edge of each eyelid.

4. Trace and cut a mouth from a scrap of felt. Put some glue around it on one side, and apply it to the doll's face. Sew around and on the middle to define it with black thread.

Voilà! I hope this will help someone.

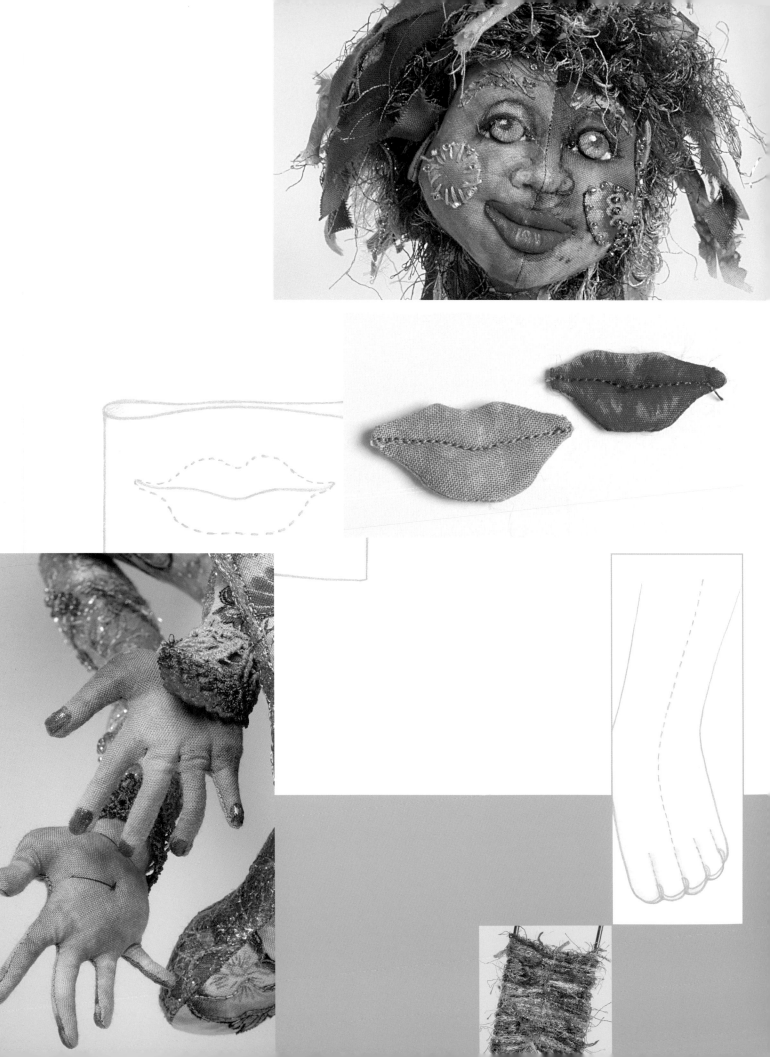

Creating with Collage

5

Life is really a huge collage. When you stop and think about all the information you collect during one day, and how you store that information until you need it, you are really creating a collage.

Some people feel they aren't "artistic" enough to create a doll, let alone the doll's face. Collage is one way a doll can be made where you "borrow" items, and place them together to create a face that doesn't have to follow any rules. This chapter will show you some ideas for collage using fabrics, beads, oil pastels, markers, and even paper.

Collage is a wonderful way to use some of those scraps of fabric, yarn, paper, and thread that you've been saving. In the previous chapters, we've been pretty serious. In this chapter we'll throw away all the specific guidelines, and have fun. You'll be surprised by the results.

Intermediate doll

Kimana is Shoshone for "butterfly." It can also mean "unchained." This seemed to fit this particular doll. She's completely unchained in her colors, her fibers, and her pose. She is made from Pattern #2 (pages 112–115).

Materials

scraps or fat quarters of various cotton fabrics: prints, batiks, plain, or hand dyed

1 fat quarter hand-dyed or batik fabric, to make the encrusted fabric

small pieces of fabric with a design (for the sample doll, I used butterfly- and floral-printed cottons)

1 fat quarter of cotton batik with a small design; this piece will be used for the appliquéd pieces

$1/4$ yard (23 cm) pieces of tulle or fine netting

miscellaneous fibers: scraps of yarn, metallic threads, embroidery threads, snippets of fabric, silk waste, and Angelina fibers

24-gauge beading wire in a color to match your theme color

good-quality stuffing

thread for machine sewing, to match fabrics

metallic and variegated rayon or polyester thread for machine work

double-sided bonding sheet (similar to Bondaweb or Wonder Under)

2 silk bridal buttons, white or off-white

artist markers in colors of your choice; Copic, Pantone, and Prismacolor all work well

Portfolio Series Water Soluble oil pastels

tissue paper

false eyelashes

seed beads, size 11, in 5 different colors

beading thread

embroidery thread

scraps of lace or trim, dyed to match your theme colors

Tools

stuffing and turning tools

beading needles

hand embroidery needles

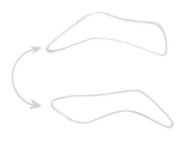

[Step 5]
Use a pencil and mark placement of eyes

[Step 10]
Eyebrows

The Face

1. Trace the two head pieces from Head #2 on the wrong side of one of your fabrics.

2. Pin this piece to a different color of fabric, right sides together.

3. Follow the directions in Chapter 3 (page 45–47) for sewing the face, turning it, and filling it with stuffing.

4. Color two silk bridal buttons for the eyes with markers in your theme color. Color one side of each button with a darker shade of the eye color. (This is the same as was done for eyes in the other chapters.) Add a pupil, and place a white dot in the side of the pupil that catches the light.

5. Mark on the face where the eyes will be placed.

6. Using strong thread, anchor at the back of the head, and come through to the marks you made. Pick up the button eyes, and sink them firmly into the face.

7. Cut out the eyelids from contrasting pieces of fabric. Follow instructions on page 49 for placing the eyelashes.

8. Edge the eyelids with glue, and place them over the eyes.

9. Iron a small piece of bonding sheet onto some scraps of fabric. These will be used for the eyebrows and for one cheek.

10. Trace the eyebrows onto the paper side of the bonding sheet. Trace one in reverse so that you have a right and a left eyebrow.

11. Cut out the eyebrows and iron them onto the face above the eyelids.

12. With embroidery thread and a straight stitch, sew the eyebrows in place.

13. Trace the lips onto the wrong side of fabric, then fold the fabric in half, right sides together.

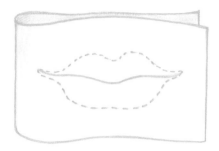

[Steps 13–14]
Trace and sew lips on wrong side of fabric

14. Sew completely around the lips. Cut them out.

15. Cut a slit on one side of the lips, toward the center. Turn them through this slit.

16. With hemostats, push out the shape of the lips. Place a small amount of stuffing in the lips.

17. Pin the lips to a piece of tissue paper. Draw the center of the mouth on the lips with a pencil.

18. Machine sew across this line. The tissue paper gives you stability, so your machine won't "eat" the lips.

19. Using the markers, color the lips by filling in with a medium red, and then use a darker red to darken the upper lip and the side of the lower lip that is in the shadow. Lighten the center with a white gel roller.

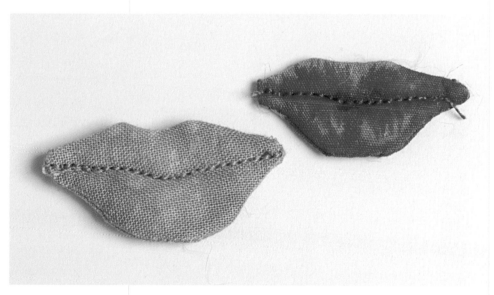

[Step 19]
Using markers, color lips

20. Pin the lips in place. Anchor a strong thread at the back of the head, and come through to the outside edge of one side of the lips. Catch the lip, go back into the head, and then go to the back of the head. Do the other side in the same way.

21. Next, go through to the center of the mouth. Catch it, and then go to the back of the head.

22. Come back to the lower lip at its center. Just catch the underneath part of the lip, and then go back to the back of the head. This anchors the lower lip, so it won't flip up some day.

23. Do the same at the center top of the upper lip.

24. To push up the cheeks a bit, take the needle from the back of the head to the inside corner of one eye.

25. Go back into the head, and down to the outside corner of the lip.

26. Go back into the head, and up to the outside corner of the head. Refer to the sculpting illustrations in Chapter 3 (page 45).

27. Do the same on the other side.

28. Sculpt the nose, following the sculpting illustrations in Chapter 3 (beginning page 45).

29. Pin the ears in place, and sew as shown in Chapter 3 (beginning page 45).

30. Add some shading to the eyes and nose with markers. Highlight the high points with a white gel roller; rub it in with your fingers as you apply it.

31. Using a white gel pen, color in the whites of the eyes.

32. Water-soluble oil pastels give a soft look to the face. Use them to add highlights to the cheekbones and the center of the nose, using colors that match the face. When you are finished, dampen them with a damp brush, or rub with a wet finger. See the close-up of the face, lower left, for this technique.

33. For the cheeks, cut out a small butterfly (or a shape of your choice) to apply to one cheek. From a piece of fabric you bonded earlier, cut a small circle. Pin the butterfly to one cheek, and the circle to the other, then iron to bond the fabrics.

34. Using embroidery thread, straight stitch the cheek in place. Add some beads along the edge of the circle cheek, and along the butterfly on the other cheek.

35. Sew a small red seed bead in the inside corner of each eye.

AUTHOR'S SUGGESTION

Another really fun way to collage a head is to use paper along with fabric, as Li Hertzi has done in this example. A cloth head was sewn and filled with stuffing. The face was painted with Liquitex Matte Gel Medium, and then covered with strips of paper that were glued to the surface with the medium. The tongue was made from cotton fabric; the underside was stitched loosely and then pulled, to make it curve. It was then sewn to the face. Small wooden beads were painted for the eyes, and paper eyelids were glued on.

Angelina fiber adds sparkle to the doll

The Body

1. Choose the fat quarter of fabric to be encrusted with embellishments. With the right side of the fabric up, throw down snippets of fabrics, yarns, threads, silk waste, and Angelina fiber onto its surface.

AUTHOR'S SUGGESTION

Angelina fibers are reminiscent of the 1950s product Angel Hair. The difference? These are made from polyester with an acrylic core rather than from spun glass, and come in a bright array of colors. Because of the poly/plastic composition of the fibers, they can be heat fixed to each other with an iron (always follow the manufacturer's instructions). Once heat fixed, they can be cut into shapes, placed between layers of other fibers, sewn to projects, or used in paper crafts. Angelina fibers add colorful opalescent effects to projects and can be mixed together to create your own color combinations— and they are available internationally.

AUTHOR'S SUGGESTION

It is best to pin this with metal-headed pins. The iron will melt plastic-headed pins.

2. On top of this, lay some tulle or thin netting. Pin it in place.

3. Place a protective sheet over the fabric. With a warm iron (set at "silk"), iron to bring out the iridescence of the Angelina fiber.

4. With your iron still on, create a beautiful embellishment with the Angelina fiber (see Author's suggestion at left).

5. Place several colors of Angelina fiber between two protective sheets (per manufacturer's instructions). Iron for about 3 seconds. Let the sheets cool, and then remove the Angelina fiber.

6. With decorative thread in the upper threader of your sewing machine, and any thread in the bobbin, free-motion sew embroidery all over the fabric. Be sure to sew closely together, as you'll be cutting out pieces of this fabric for parts of the body and surface embellishments.

7. Iron one side of the double-sided bonding sheet to the wrong side of the printed fabrics. (The sample doll uses butterfly and pansy prints.)

8. Cut out several of these. Peel off the paper backing, and place them on the fabric.

9. Iron to set.

10. With decorative thread in your sewing machine, sew a straight stitch around the appliqués.

11. On the wrong side of this fabric, trace the Body Front. Cut out with pinking shears.

12. Trace the Body Back, Arms, and Legs onto the wrong side of the rest of this fabric.

13. To make right and left arms and legs, reverse the pattern as you trace.

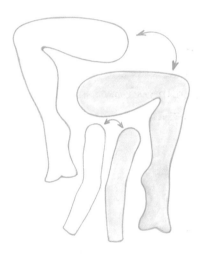

[Step 13]
Reverse one leg and arm when tracing on fabric

14. Pin the body pieces to the encrusted fabric.

15. Sew down Seam # 3 on the Body Back, leaving open where marked.

16. Finish the body as shown in Chapter 3 (pages xx).

17. The hands are traced and sewn on two pieces of hand-dyed fabrics in contrasting colors. To make a right hand and a left hand, reverse the pattern when tracing. Each side of the hand will be a different fabric.

18. Follow the instructions in Chapter 3 (page 43), for putting the hands together and attaching them to the arms.

[Step 17]
Use different fabrics for each side of the hands

[Step 6]
Sew along center of wrapped yarns to create hair

Finishing

1. Place the head on the neck as described in Chapter 3 (page 44).

2. It is best to apply the hair to this doll before putting on the arms and legs. The hair is made with torn pieces of fabric, yarn, and Angelina fiber (see page 98 for more on Angelina fiber). You will use the ironed Angelina in Step 5.

3. Cut out several strips that measure 6" x ½" (15 x 1.3 cm).

4. Cut and tear several pieces of fabric that measure 6" x ⅜" (15 x 1 cm).

5. Start machine sewing the strips together by laying down strips of fabric, cut pieces of yarn, and some of the Angelina. This piece will be 8" (20 cm) long. Set aside.

6. Wrap a yarn of your choice around a coat hanger that you have bent into a long "U" shape (left). It needs to be bent so that it is 2½" (6.3 cm) wide.

7. Sew down the center of this . You'll need a finished piece 16" (41 cm) long.

8. Remove from the wire.

9. Wrap this piece around the head, and pin it in place. Leave room at the center back, toward the top, for the longer piece you sewed earlier. Hand sew this to the head.

10. Hand sew a gathering stitch along the center of the long piece created in Step 5, and pull it into a bundle. Pin this at the center of the head, and hand sew in place.

11. Add some larger pieces of cut Angelina to the hair.

12. Close up the openings in the legs. Adjust the body to the desired position. The sample doll has one leg bent, as if she were sitting on the floor. The other leg is sewn so that she can hold it with her hands.

13. Once you are satisfied with the placement, hand sew the legs in place.

14. The arms are first embellished, and then sewn to the body. Using some pieces of hand-dyed lace or trim, cover the raw seams where the hands are sewn to the arms. Pin these in place, and hand sew with matching thread.

15. The sample doll's right arm is hand embroidered. Use a blanket stitch (see page 109) to sew around the butterfly and flower. A stem stitch runs up the arm, with seed beads sewn here and there to add sparkle. Cut a small piece of the Angelina that has been heat set, and sew it to the body with embroidery thread and a blanket stitch. Add seed beads along the edge. Hand sew this arm to the body.

16. If you wish, sculpt the toes. First, use a white pencil to draw the placement of the toes.

17. Using matching thread and a small needle, anchor the thread underneath the foot. Come up between the "toes" you have marked, and do a back and forth stitch, starting from the top of the foot, and continuing back to the back of the foot. Repeat stitch the length of the toes.

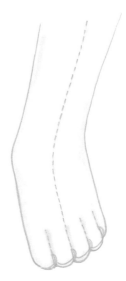

[Steps 16–19]
Draw in toes, then hand sew to sculpt and define them

18. When you get close to the end of the foot, wrap the thread from the top to the back, and around the end. This rounds out the toes and creates separation.

19. After the last toe is sculpted, anchor the thread in the bottom of the foot and cut the loose end.

20. Add some more beads to her body, if you wish.

You have now created several wonderful dolls with various faces. You may be like me, in that there are certain techniques I prefer over others. All are fun, and all have their uses.

Gemini

LYNNE SWARD

The artist writes:

With my studio overflowing with fabric, the task of choosing the right fabrics for Gemini was daunting at first. The layered, fringed skirt and shoulder treatments came from a small, unfinished purse. One of my design styles involves sewing rows of straight stitching with coordinated rayon threads on top of a piece of fabric. I pinned a variation of Patti's body pattern on the machine-embellished fabric, and machine zigzag stitched around the edge of the shape. I left the top of the head and the bottom of the body open.

My favorite part of doll making is the head. My faces are usually flat, so I was thrilled that Patti wanted me to work on the beginning doll pattern. I cut out the appropriate tiny shapes for the eyes, nose, and mouth from graphic patterns I saw in my fabric stash. I fused these onto fusible web (like Wonder Under). These are cut out, and ironed on the face fabric. The features are machine zigzag stitched or satin stitched around the edges.

Lastly, the face is machine satin stitched along the main fabric. The hair is applied as the last step. The head opening hasn't been closed yet, because I hand sew yarns into the opening, and then close it up.

Jillian

SANDRA SIMMONS

The artist writes:

In deciding upon a collage approach for making Jillian, I decided to use fabric collage to create the body. First, I created crazy-quilted fabric from brightly colored batik fabrics, with decorative stitching along the seams. I wanted to add some sparkle, so I used gold metallic thread for free-motion embroidery on top of the crazy-quilted fabric. Beadwork was then added to Jillian's bag, along the flap and shoulder straps, to add interest as well as texture.

The face, hands, and feet were created from hand-dyed fabric in order to provide a skin tone of color. For the face, I took a very standard approach, using the graft method for placement of features. I then penciled them in using a mechanical pencil. Next, I outlined the eyes, eyelid area, the sides of the nose, and the lip area with a brown Pigma pen to give the features more definition and permanency. At this point, I needle sculpted the face using a quilt-weight thread and a 3" (7.6 cm) needle.

After the needle sculpting was complete, I colored the face by using various shades of green for the eyes, and crimsons for the cheeks and lips. A brown Pigma pen was then used to add more definition, place the eyelashes, and draw the eyebrows. Shading was added with sienna and brown tones along the sides of the eyes, nose, mouth, and temple area. Highlights were then placed near the shaded areas, along the nose, and on the bottom potion of the lip, using a cream-colored pencil. A white gel pen was used for highlighting the eyes. After all the coloring was complete, the face was sealed using Createx Textile Medium, and heat set, using a very small Clover iron.

Liala of Ahtrarrath

MICHELLE MEINHOLD

The artist writes:

Liala of Ahtrarrath comes from the lost city of Atlantis. The harmony of colors in her billowing pants and the vines of flowers along her hair and arms are reminiscent of how peaceful the city of Atlantis once was.

I started the head by first creating it per Patti's instructions, then adding some line drawings of what I wanted to bead embroider. Once that was done, I completed her coloration, and started the beadwork. I used some basic bead embroidery stitches; they consisted of couching the beadwork and making some bead picots. I was able to use some vintage Swarovski crystals that I had been saving for something special.

Once her head was beaded, the rest of the doll fell into place. She didn't want to wear too many pieces of clothing, which might detract from her face and the butterfly on her back, so I was left with making her a pair of harem pants, and adjusting her arms for modesty. I carried the flower theme to the vines that went from her hair down and around her arms. That seemed to work for her.

She was definitely a labor of love. I was able to break out of my safe zone when it came to the beading, and expand my skills with the bead embroidery that was needed on her face and on her back.

Wide Open

LI HERTZI

The artist writes:

Because I wanted a standing doll, I straightened one leg, inserted a dowel, and stuffed it. Using my trusty glue gun, I wrapped some bumpy yarn around the doll in places, placed some of my grandmother's old lace strategically here and there (kept in place with the glue gun), crinkled up some paper and put that on, and then put the little glass things on the hands.

I used Natural Sand Texture Gel (from Liquitex) and applied it thickly over the textured parts, and some on the open spaces. Onto that I sprinkled sand, and "smooshed" in fine pumice gel for making pastel paper. I let that dry overnight, and through the next scalding "SoCal" day. Then I used Scribbles dimensional fabric writer to draw the lines and create the dots. That always takes a while to dry, so I left it overnight too. I painted all the parts with gesso and let that dry. (There was a lot of drying!)

Next I painted her mostly blue, but it was too much; it brought me down, sending my wide-open feeling into the cyan paint pot of melancholy. So I painted the face yellow, added the yellow on the leg, and then just let the brush lead me. Here and there I added words and some pictures cut from a laser print. I have to say, I had more fun just painting along than anything else. I added the beads and hair with the glue gun, and then covered the whole thing in Behr Polyurethane.

The best part of this doll was going to the large home-improvement store with her in pieces and getting the young whippersnapper to help me find the right wing nuts to attach the appendages!

Raggedy Does Vegas

ANNE MAYER HESSE

The artist writes:

To begin, I drew a Raggedy face on muslin that was then sewn into a round pancake-type face. This was lightly filled with stuffing. Following the drawn lines, I filled the face using bead embroidery. When the face was completed, the doll was assembled, and the face was sewn onto the head of the doll.

Bead embroidery is simply laying down a row of beads and couching (catching) the beads to the surface with the same needle and thread. By changing the colors to follow the design, the face emerges in all its shining glory.

To emphasize the beaded face, I beaded hair around the head using a bead technique called simple fringe. I then added marabou and ostrich "hair."

The name for my doll came from the little dice I added throughout the costuming. As many doll makers can attest, the doll always lets us know who she is!

Esther

RIVKAH TZEVVA

The artist writes:

Having met Patti through the Internet, I was excited when she asked me to make a doll for this book. Sculpting dolls faces is my favorite part of doll making. For Esther's face, I chose a knit fabric, similar to T-shirt fabric. I like working with this medium because it allows easy definition to the face. I like working with clay as well and decided to use it for her eyes. I shaped them, then baked them to harden the clay. The eyes were colored using paints and pens. While the eyes were drying, I sculpted the face with needle and thread. Generally, I do pretty dolls, but I felt this doll needed more character.

After most of her features were sculpted, I inserted the eyes and set them in the face by adding fabric eyelids. Her eyelashes were created with peacock feathers hand sewn to the edges. The lips were drawn with colored pencils and fabric pens. Her hair was hand sewn to her head after her clothing was made and put on the body. Esther holds a harp and plays to soothe the king's nerves.

Claudia (Beginning doll, #1, p. 22)

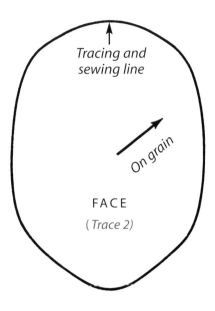

Tracing and
sewing line

On grain

FACE
(Trace 2)

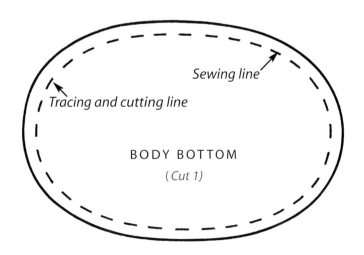

Sewing line

Tracing and cutting line

BODY BOTTOM
(Cut 1)

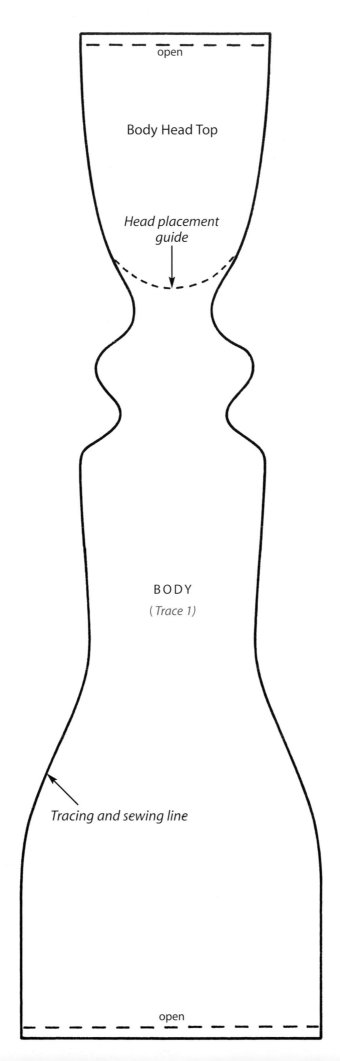

open

Body Head Top

*Head placement
guide*

BODY
(*Trace 1*)

Tracing and sewing line

open

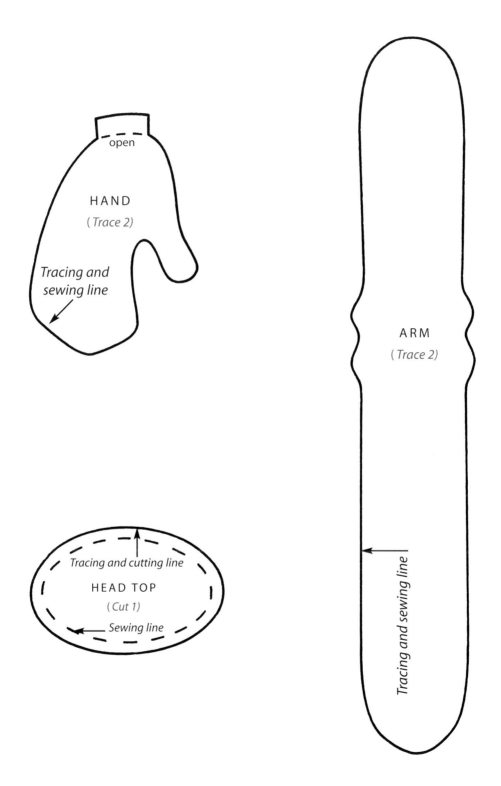

open

HAND

(Trace 2)

Tracing and sewing line

ARM

(Trace 2)

Tracing and cutting line

HEAD TOP

(Cut 1)

Sewing line

Tracing and sewing line

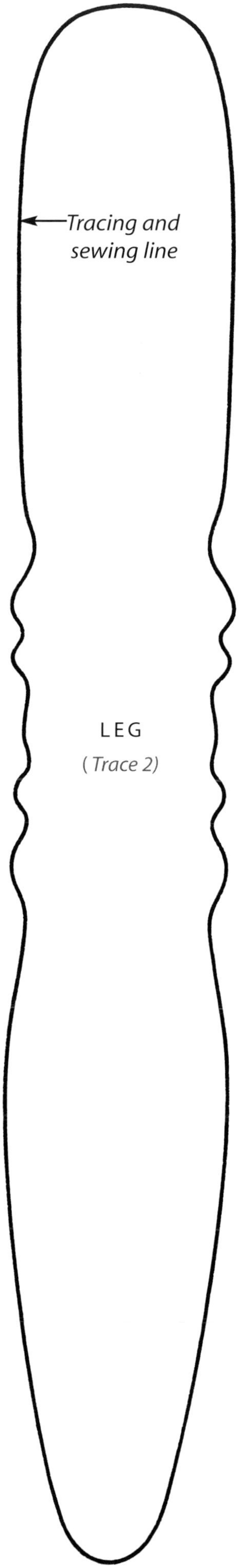

← *Tracing and*
sewing line

LEG

(*Trace 2*)

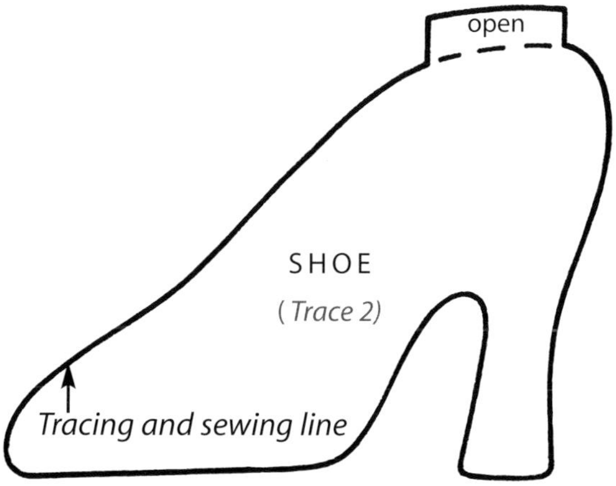

open

SHOE

(*Trace 2*)

↑
Tracing and sewing line

Tania (Intermediate doll, #2, p. 40)

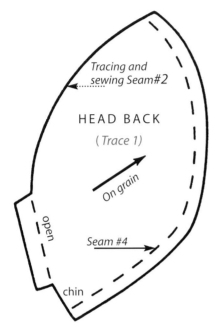

Tracing and sewing Seam #2

HEAD BACK
(Trace 1)

On grain

open

Seam #4

chin

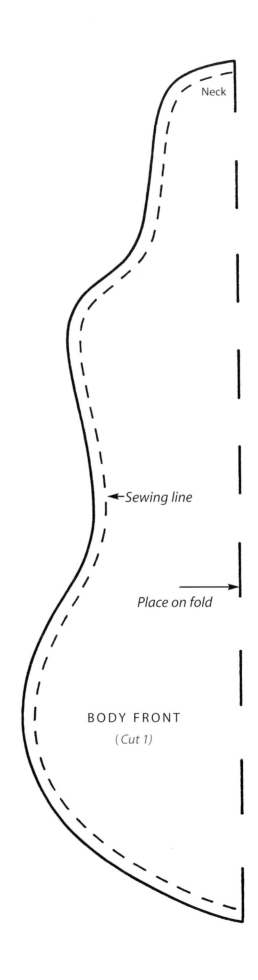

Neck

←Sewing line

Place on fold →

BODY FRONT
(Cut 1)

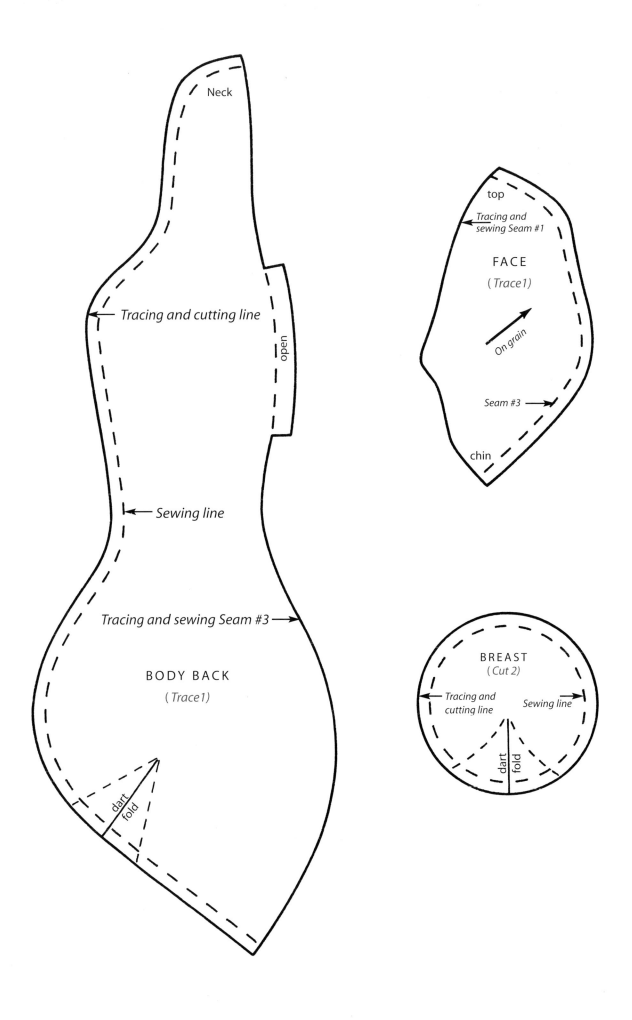

Neck

Tracing and cutting line

open

Sewing line

Tracing and sewing Seam #3 →

BODY BACK
(Trace1)

dart fold

top

Tracing and sewing Seam #1

FACE
(Trace1)

On grain

Seam #3 →

chin

BREAST
(Cut 2)

← Tracing and cutting line

Sewing line →

dart fold

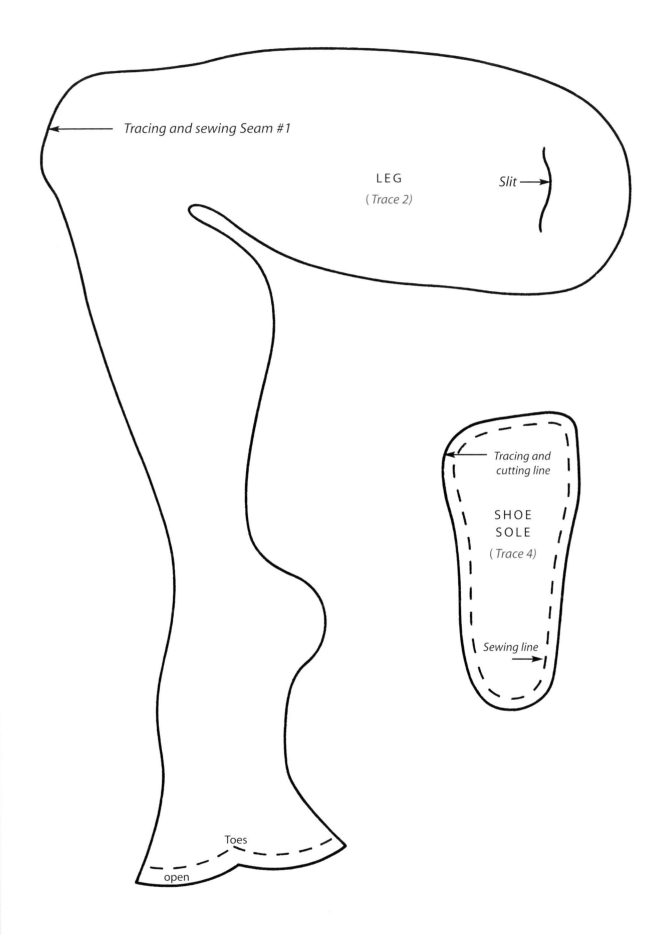

Tracing and sewing Seam #1

LEG
(Trace 2)

Slit ➝

Tracing and
cutting line

SHOE
SOLE
(Trace 4)

Sewing line ➝

Toes

open

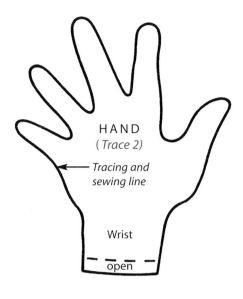

HAND
(*Trace 2*)

← *Tracing and
sewing line*

Wrist

open

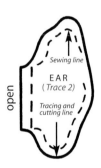

Sewing line

open

EAR
(*Trace 2*)

*Tracing and
cutting line*

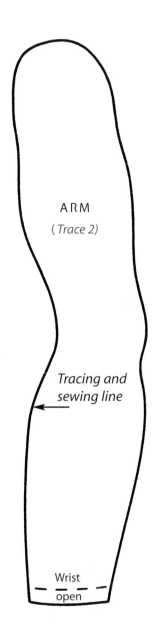

ARM
(*Trace 2*)

*Tracing and
sewing line*

Wrist

open

Tracing and sewing line

EYELID
(*Trace 4)*

Magdalene (Advanced doll, #3, p. 64)

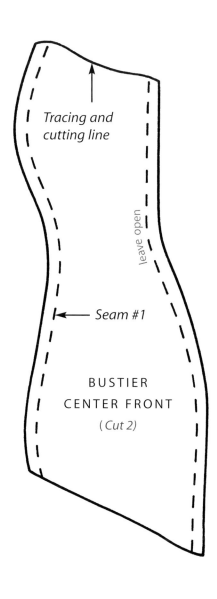

Tracing and
cutting line

leave open

Seam #1

BUSTIER
CENTER FRONT
(Cut 2)

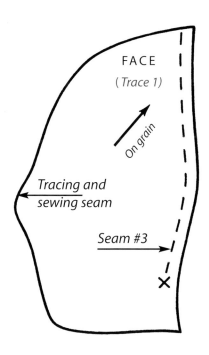

FACE
(Trace 1)

On grain

Tracing and
sewing seam

Seam #3

✕

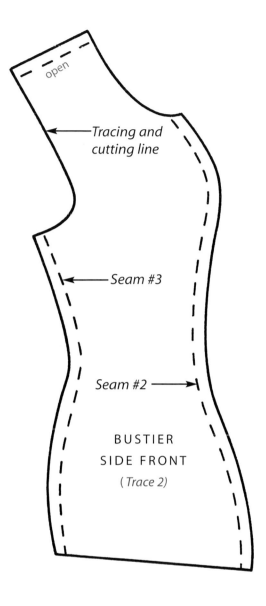

open

Tracing and cutting line

Seam #3

Seam #2

BUSTIER
SIDE FRONT

(*Trace 2*)

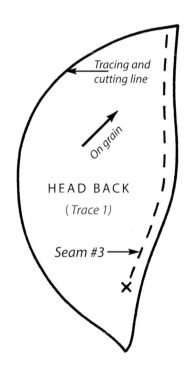

Tracing and cutting line

On grain

HEAD BACK

(*Trace 1*)

Seam #3

✕

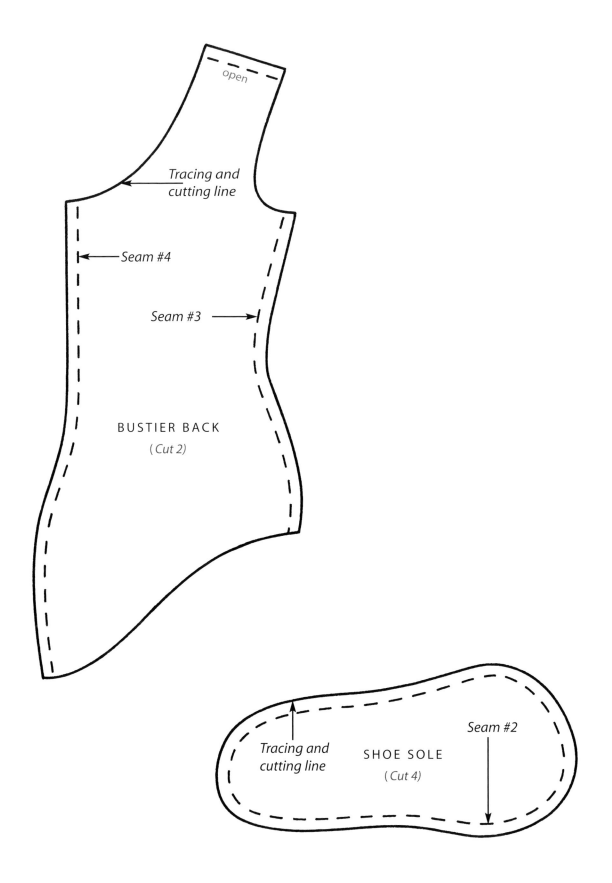

open

*Tracing and
cutting line*

Seam #4

Seam #3

BUSTIER BACK
(*Cut 2*)

*Tracing and
cutting line*

SHOE SOLE
(*Cut 4*)

Seam #2

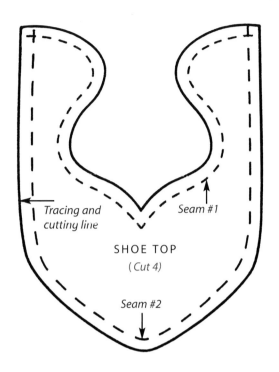

Tracing and
cutting line

Seam #1

SHOE TOP
(Cut 4)

Seam #2

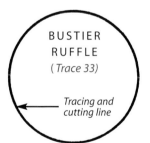

BUSTIER
RUFFLE
(Trace 33)

Tracing and
cutting line

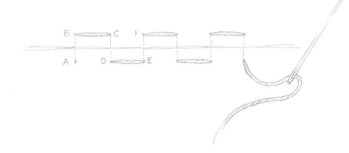

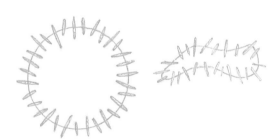

Embroidery Stitches

Ladder Stitch

1. Stitch down from the front of the piece at A.

2. Hiding the thread, go into the neck, coming out at B.

3. Run the needle over the fabric for a bit, and then insert needle through fabric at C.

4. Run the needle under the fabric, and come out at D.

5. Go back into the lower section at E. Run the needle under the fabric, and come out at E.

6. Continue until the seam is finished.

Straight Stitch

1. Come up from the back of the appliqué, along the edge.

2. Go into the appliqué in a straight line.

3. Continue stitching around the appliqué in this manner.

   Straight stitches can be worked irregularly or uniformly, depending on the effect you wish to achieve.

Blanket Stitch

1. Bring the thread to the front at A. Take the needle to the back at B, and come up at C with the needle over the working thread.

2. Repeat this stitch along the edge of the appliqué.

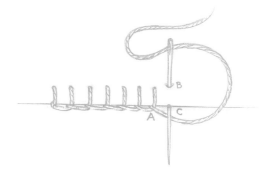

Stem Stitch

1. Bring needle to the front of the fabric at A.

2. With the thread below the needle, take it back into the fabric at B, and out slightly to the right of A.

3. Pull the thread to set the first stitch. Insert the needle at C, keeping the thread below the needle.

4. Work this stitch from left to right, taking regular small stitches along the line of the design.

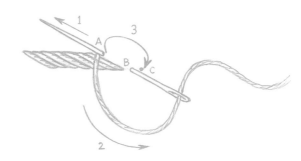

Resources

United States

Art Doll Quarterly
22992 Millcreek, Suite B
Laguna Hills, CA 92653
877-STAMPER
www.artdollquarterly.com

Caravan Beads
915 Forest Ave.
Portland, ME 04103
207-761-2503
www.caravanbeads.com

Complete line of beads; retail and wholesale

Cloth Doll Connection
www.clothdollconnection.com

Online doll-making classes, links, and a calendar of events

Doll Heaven
Lisa Risler
2590 FM 356
Trinity, TX 75862
936-594-6703
www.lisasheaven.com
lisarisler@runbox.com

All your doll supply needs: mohair, patterns, paints, online classes, and more

Dollmakers Journey
www.DollmakersJourney.com

Patterns, books, and supplies for the contemporary doll artist

Joggles, Inc.
www.joggles.com

Patterns, fabrics, books, mohair, and other fibers

Meinke Toy
PMB #411
55 E. Long Lake Road
Troy, MI 48085
www.meinketoy.com

Books, threads, stabilizers, and Angelina fiber

PMC Designs
9019 Stargaze Avenue
San Diego, CA 92129
858-484-5118
www.pmcdesigns.com
patti@pmcdesigns.com

*Patterns, tools, newsletters, classes, and
one-of-a-kind dolls*

Quilting Arts Magazine
Cloth Paper Scissors Magazine
23 Gleasondale Road
P. O. Box 685
Stow, MA 01775
www.quiltingarts.com

Robertsons' Enterprises
Box 357
Dolores, CO 81323
970-882-3389

Catalog of hard-to-find cloth doll supplies

Rupert Gibbon & Spider
P. O. Box 425
Healdsburg, CA 95448
800-442-0455
www.jacquardproducts.com

*Jacquard products: Dye-Na-Flow, Lumiere,
and textile paints*

Textura Trading Company
866-698-6989
www.texturatrading.com

Angelina fiber, yarns, silk fibers

Tsukineko, Inc.
17640 NE 65th Street
Redmond, WA 98052
425-883-7733
www.tsukineko.com

Fantastix, stamp pads

Canada

Opus Framing & Arts
www.opusframing.com

Jacquard products, books, and workshops

Australia

Anne's Glory Box
60-62 Beaumont Street
Hamilton
NSW 2303
+61 049 61 6016
www.annesglorybox.com.au

*Fabrics, dyes, paints, beads, books, stabilizers,
and mohair*

The Thread Studio
6 Smith Street
Perth
Western Australia 6000
+61 8 9227 1561
www.thethreadstudio.com

Threads, stabilizers, paints, books, and online classes

Yadeno Fibre Craft
35 Lake Drive
Meringandan
Queensland 4352
+61 07 6496 9329
www.yadenofibrecraft.com.au

United Kingdom

Art Van Go
1 Stevenage Road
Knebworth
Herts SG3 6AN
+44 01438 814946
www.artvango.co.uk

Jacquard products, Stewart Gill Paints, and books

Crafty Notions
P. O. Box 6141
Newark NG24 2FQ
+44 01636 659890
www.craftynotions.com

Stabilizers, paints, Angelina fibers, beads and bead supplies, and books

Fibrecrafts & George Weil
Old Portsmouth Rd.
Peasmarsh, Guildford, Surrey
GU3 1LZ
www.fibrecrafts.com

Paints, Angelina fibers, books, and workshops

The Yorkshire Art Store
10 Market Place
Picering, North Yorkshire YO 187AA
0800 195 7440
www.yorkshireartstore.co.uk

Jacquard products, paints, and books

Europe

Rougier et Ple
13/15 Boulevard des Filles du Calvaire
75003 Paris
France
+33 01 44 54 81 00
www.crea.tm.fr

Colored pencils, pastels, paints, and craft supplies

Sennelier
3 quai Voltaire
75007 Paris
France
www.magasinsennelier.com/anglais/welcome.htm

Colored pencils, oil pastels, paints, and fine art supplies

Zijdelings
Karina van Vught
Kapelstraat 93
5046 CL Tilburg
The Netherlands
www.zijdelings.com

Jacquard products, books, fabrics, and workshops

Further Reading

Creative Cloth Doll Making
Patti Medaris Culea
Rockport Publishers
ISBN 1-56496-942-8

Collage for the Soul
Holly Harrison
Rockport Publishers
ISBN 1-56496-962-2

Painters' Wild Workshop
Lynn Leon Loscutoff
Rockport Publishers
ISBN 1-56496-434-5

Basic Portrait Techniques
Rachel Wolf
North Light Books
ISBN 0-89134-552-3

Contributing Artists

Shawn Asiala
269 NE 17th Street
Delray Beach, FL 33444
USA
561-272-6458
shawnasiala@bellsouth.net

[handwritten: 524 East a Hawter Ave]

Since childhood, Shawn Asiala has adored dolls. Her father, a USAF officer, traveled around the world, collecting beautiful handmade dolls for Shawn from many countries. Before she was eight, Shawn began sewing clothes on a Singer Featherweight. She soon loved it, and quickly moved on to other sewing projects.

Shawn lives with her loving husband Tom and beautiful daughter Jenny. She works and teaches at Quilters Marketplace in Delray Beach, Florida. To share her love of doll making, Shawn is a member of an inspirational South Florida doll club called the Sandollr's.

J. Arley Berryhill
1800 N. Green Valley Parkway #1412
Henderson, NV 89074
USA
702-361-5964
arleyberryhill@aol.com
www.arleyberryhill.com

Arley Berryhill has been making dolls, both cloth and clay, for ten years. With a background in art, design, theater, fashion, and costuming, he feels all his skills are being utilized in doll making. For the past twenty-five years, Arley has made a living creating costumes, props, masks, and jewelry for television, stage, commercials, and film. He's worked on costumes for Broadway shows, including *The Phantom of the Opera*, puppets for the Jim Henson Muppet Shop, and headdresses for the Ringling Bros. Circus. He spent five years making hats, armor, and accessories for the Seattle Opera Company, and recently worked on costumes for Disneyland and Universal Studios. Arley now lives near Las Vegas, and is in charge of wardrobe for a hotel show.

Heather Cooper
20 Forrest Street
South Perth 6151, Western Australia
Australia
hcooper@nedkelly.net.au

After reading Julia Cameron's book *The Artist's Way*, and making hundreds of dolls based on the work of other cloth doll artists, Heather Cooper started creating her own designs. To enrich her doll-making skills, Heather has attended cloth-doll-making conferences in Australia and completed Module 1 of the Thread Studio's machine embroidery workshop over the Internet.

Opportunities to exhibit her dolls throughout Australia, Japan (Quilt Week Yokohama 2000), and at the Knitting and Stitching Show in London have opened the door for Heather in teaching her techniques and selling her patterns. She now has twelve original designs in pattern form.

Sherry Goshon
2036 Monniger Road
Albion, IA 50005
USA
641-488-2450
innerchildslg@yahoo.com

At home working in any medium, Sherry Goshon is one of the gifted few who prefers to sculpt in cloth. She loves the warm, soft feel that textiles give her dolls. Sherry started sewing on her grandmother's lap as a young child. She is an intuitive, self-taught artist, and chooses fabrics as much by feel as by look. Sherry's art has been featured in many magazines, books, and exhibits. She is past president of ODACA (Original Doll Artist Council of America), and is one of the most popular teachers of the art of the doll in the United States, Canada, Europe, and Australia.

Li Hertzi
300 Carlsbad Village Drive #108A-272
Carlsbad, CA 92008
USA
760-431-0870 (x 102)
lihertzi@lihertzidesign.com
www.lihertzidesign.com

Li Hertzi is an artist, designer, computer adventurer, teacher, and maker of decidedly funky dolls. She grew up on a farm in Greentown, Ohio, land of wide landscapes, white farm houses, lakes, and weather that leads you to look inward for light.

She studied at Parsons School of Design and the New School, both in New York City. She is interested in the figure as an icon, with a focus on the basic sculptural elements found in African, Pre-Columbian, Native American, and primitive art. By creating patterns, she invites everyone to play in the richness of the creative experiment, and to be amused in the process.

Anne Mayer Hesse
1032 Palmetto Drive
Richmond, KY 40475
USA
859-623-2455
anniedolls@adelphia.net

Anne Mayer Hesse has been making art since the early 1970s, but it wasn't until the 1980s that her focus turned to figurative work. Anne's background is in education. She holds a B.S. in English and an M.Ed. in Special Education. Anne followed her creative visions, and with little art training, has created one-of-a-kind art dolls. Anne is sought after worldwide to teach her techniques in fiber and bead arts.

Angela Jarecki
1705 McArthur Street
Blue Springs, MO 64015
USA
ajareck1@comcast.net

Angela Jarecki was a greeting-card artist with Hallmark Cards for ten years. She now freelances for them and other card and publishing companies. Angela has always loved dolls, fibers, fabrics, yarn, beads, and embellishments of all kinds. She had lots of creative "stuff" in her stash but no real direction until about five years ago, when she found the fantastic world of doll making. She has taught art classes for children, creativity workshops for adults, and several Internet classes on making dolls. Angela lives outside of Kansas City, Missouri, with her husband and four children.

Kris Knutzen
3019 Riverview Drive
Fairbanks, AK 99709
USA
koinc@ptialaska.net

Kris, a twenty-five-year resident of Fairbanks, Alaska, started making dolls three years ago. She has always been artistic, but couldn't settle into a particular medium until she discovered cloth dolls. A dark, cold winter and an opportunity to take a doll class were the beginning of her cloth doll passion. Kris helped start a thriving cloth doll group in Fairbanks called the SoBad Art Doll Club. Various teachers and the "good girlfriends" from SoBad have taught Kris to think beyond the box—as is very evident in her contribution to this book.

Jacquie Lecuyer
130 Queen Elizabeth Drive #201
Ottawa, ON
Canada K2P 1E6
jacquiesew@sympatico.ca
www.offthefloordolls.com

Jacquie Lecuyer has been making dolls for the past twelve years. She started teaching her doll-making techniques a little more than two years ago. She's the president of her local doll guild, All Dolled Up. One of Jacquie's dolls was the winner of the first soft doll competition of the Canadian Doll Artist Association.

Allison Marano
3516 Emerson Avenue
Erie, PA 16508
USA
814-864-0556
allison@faewyckstudios.com
www.faewyckstudios.com

Alllson Marano holds a B.A. In FIne Art and Design, and worked as a graphic artist and illustrator for years before shifting her focus to cloth doll making. A local psychologist asked her to design and make a "soft" doll that he could use in therapy, and an obsession was born. Her work has appeared in *Art Doll Quarterly* and is currently featured in several U.S. galleries. She resides in Erie, Pennsylvania, with her husband and three sons.

Michelle Meinhold
1750 E. Brandon Lane
Fresno, CA 93720
USA
559-434-8434
meinhold@csufresno.edu
www.michellemeinhold.com

Michelle Meinhold discovered her love for color while studying fine arts at the University of California, Santa Cruz. The color choices available in textiles and beads have helped fuel her creative fires. At first she used beads just to embellish her dolls. But one day, obsession took over, and beads became her medium of choice. Michelle still makes cloth dolls to satisfy her need to create. Her line of Floral Tassel dolls came into bloom when she wanted to combine the dolls with beads. She has been a cloth doll artist since 1985, and has been teaching cloth dolls and beading since 1998.

Shashi Nayagam
35 Honeypots Road
Mayford, Woking
Surrey, GU22 9QW
UK
shashi.nayagam@ntlworld.com

Shashi Nayagam was born and raised in a small hill station in India. It was there that she met a friend of her mother's who made cloth dolls. As a child, Shashi spent many hours looking at these beautiful dolls. She dreamed of someday making her own dolls. After growing up, getting married, and moving to England, Shashi decided to make her dream of doll making come true. With the help of the Internet and online classes, she developed her own style of doll making. Drawing and painting were among Shashi's favorite childhood pastimes. She is now able to use those skills in creating beautiful dolls.

Irene Pichard
"Pau," Commune de St. Pierre d'Albigny
73250 Savoie
France
Marc.Thierry.pich@wanadoo.fr

Irene Pichard was born in Africa, and moved to France when she was sixteen. She is married, and has four children and one grandson. She began to sew, knit, and crochet when she was twenty years old, and hasn't quit crafting since. Two years ago, Irene began to do research on the Internet, looking for cloth doll making sites. She discovered that there was a "cloth doll world," and since then has been "totally addicted." After making other designers' dolls, Irene has started designing her own. Irene said that she never had a passion before, but now "I know that it's like a very good medication that allows one to endure the bad ways of life."

Kandy Scott
300 Luman Road #87
Phoenix, OR 97535
USA
541-535-2090
kandyscott@earthlink.net

Born and raised in Oregon, Kandy Scott began her creative life as a hair dresser, then moved into the fiber arts. She and a partner started a pattern design business in the 1980s and traveled throughout the United States, Australia, and New Zealand. Today, Kandy prefers teaching to designing her own patterns, as motivating others to create has become a passion of hers. Her classes are inspiring because she believes there are no mistakes, just creative readjustments.

Sandra Simmons
3895 MacIntosh Drive
Columbus, OH 43230
USA
614-476-3342
raggedysan@aol.com

Sandra Simmons has always had a love for art. She remembers drawing and painting from a very young age, and as a teenager was especially drawn to the world of fashion design. After exploring a gamut of art-related interests, she started realizing her love for textures, colors, and then textiles. She soon knew that her primary interests were those in the fiber arts.

Sandra discovered doll making through a magazine article about elinor peace bailey that showcased many of elinor's dolls. It was this article that spurred her desire to one day to create and surround herself with such delightful characters. She soon found a class that elinor taught, and it was absolute bliss. Sandra's love for doll making was just beginning.

Judy Skeel
6881 Tussic Street Road
Westerville, OH 43082
USA
www.skeelhaven.com
skeelhaven1@yahoo.com

Born and raised in central Ohio, Judy Skeel has been creating art in a wide range of media all her life. She also gardens, and writes poetry and stories. Judy, her wonderful firefighter husband, and two sons named their home Skeelhaven, and always sign handmade gifts, "With Love From Skeelhaven." This became the name of Judy's business. Living with three males and being surrounded by testosterone, the artist says she needed something feminine in her life. She turned her artistic skills toward dolls, and discovered an incredible new world that has combined all her art forms for one purpose: creating art dolls.

Karen Smith
6801 Cloudcroft Lane
Anchorage, AK 99516
USA
momarchy@yahoo.com

Sewing has been a long-time love of artist Karen Smith. She makes most of her own clothes, and clothing for her two sons and daughters. Karen fell into doll making when her mom, who collected antique dolls, asked her to make some doll clothes. The first cloth doll she made came from a magazine, and the pattern had to be enlarged by drawing it on a grid. This started her on her journey into cloth doll making.

In 1976, three days after their wedding, Karen and her husband moved to Anchorage, Alaska, from Southern California. She writes, "The long, dark days of winter have helped me create dolls, and experiment with different techniques."

Lynne Sward
625 Bishop Drive
Virginia Beach, VA 23455
USA
757-497-7917
l5s4w38@rcn.com

For Lynne Sward, teaching and designing dolls go together like "peanut butter and jelly." Just ask anyone who has taken any of Lynne's classes. Because of her fascination with faces, she is constantly researching new materials and techniques to develop unique ideas for her nontraditional dolls. Lynne loves sharing this research with anyone who will listen.

Lynne's work has been exhibited in juried and invitational shows around the United States, Canada, England, and Japan. Besides making "things," Lynne has a fascination with spiritual philosophies, tribal cultures, art history, botany, movies, and family. These interests influence much of the art she loves and creates.

Laly Tapia
Constancio Vigil #130
Las Condes, Santiago
Chile
lalytap@hotmail.com
www.laly.cl

Laly Tapia was born in Iquique, in northern Chile. As soon as she was old enough to handle the tools, she started making dolls. Being married to an Air Force pilot and living in England, Spain, and South Africa introduced her to many ways of doll making. A friend brought her a U.S. magazine that featured dolls made from panty hose, using a technique called soft sculpture. This piqued Laly's enthusiasm, and since 1983 she's been developing that technique in her own style. In Chile, she was the first to teach this technique; as Laly says, she was the pioneer in her country. With two daughters and six grandchildren, Laly has had much practice making dolls. She teaches doll making and has participated in doll competitions in the United States.

Robyn Trefry
54 Holmes Street
Shelley, Western Australia 6168
Australia
rtrefry@hotmail.com

Robyn Trefry started making dolls in the mid- to late 1980s from patterns in magazines, and from U.S. mail-order sources. While living in the Netherlands in the late 1990s, Robyn was introduced to self-hardening clays and doll costuming. Since returning to her native Australia, her love of using cloth has grown. Robyn designs her own dolls and has a line of patterns.

Rivkah Tzevva
Dolls of Valor
POB 380
Tzfat 13100
Israel
Rivkah70@netvision.net.il

Rivkah lives in a beautiful town near the Sea of Galilee. The town is full of artists and has been a source of inspiration for her art. She started out sewing clothing at a young age. Teachers throughout her school years saw her talent and encouraged her to study various art forms. Ceramics and portrait painting were her favorites. Doll making came to Rivkah through her volunteer service in her community. She introduced simple doll making techniques to the children at the community center. This has evolved into a full-time career. She now designs her own cloth dolls and has started a website to promote local artists in Israel.

Judi Wellnitz
3462 Durham Circle
North Pole, Alaska 99705
USA
Ak_icecube@yahoo.com

Judi lives in North Pole, Alaska, which actually does have a sunny season! But the long winters are just perfect for doll making. She's been making dolls for about three years. She found a soft doll and animal magazine and ended up totally obsessed. She is connected to the doll world through the Internet, allowing her to learn from other doll makers around the world.

Acknowledgments

Unless you have written a book, it's impossible to fully understand how important other people are in getting the project from brainstorm to bookstore. My first book, *Creative Cloth Doll Making*, was a collaboration of family, friends, artists, and the publishing team at Rockport. Ditto for *Creative Cloth Doll Faces*.

Never underestimate what happens in your childhood—the genesis of my books. My parents, Bob and Fran Medaris, always encouraged me to follow my artistic dreams, and develop my God-given talent.

Through the years, I have rubbed shoulders and broken sewing needles with many gifted artists. My dear friend Karen "Purple Lady" Wooton saw my potential beyond making Raggedy Ann dolls, and helped me move into doll designing. Thank you, Karen, for your heart of Alexandrite.

As you read this book, you will see the creative genius of doll makers and artists from around the world. I am humbled by each of these well-known and gracious people who enthusiastically said "Yes!" when I asked them if they would create dolls for the book.

The people at Rockport Publishers are rock solid in their support and professionalism. Thanks to Mary Ann Hall, who asked me to do another book. She was in my corner with gentle suggestions and brilliant editing skills. During the development of my book, she delivered a beautiful baby girl. When it came time for Mary Ann to focus on her baby, Rochelle Bourgault came off the bench to keep me in the game.

Judy Love took my illustrations and made them sing. I love her work! I so appreciated the wonderful work of Roberta Frauwirth, who made my patterns more symmetrical (we all know some of us artists are anything but symmetrical!). Thanks also to Bob Hirsch, a brilliant San Diego photographer who understood my ideas and made them come to life.

On the home front, my husband John kept me from going completely bonkers. In his "spare time" he took care of my pattern orders, answered many of my emails, and did the laundry and grocery shopping. The introduction in this book reflects my thoughts; however, it was John who got inside my head and put the words on paper. He knows me so well that he was able to express in words what I have never been able to fully tell others.

To all who have read this book, I hope you are still wearing happy faces. Here's looking at you, friends.

About the Author

Patti Medaris Culea studied art in Los Angeles and Japan and began her career as a painter and portrait artist. Her interest in the human figure evolved into working with cloth. Today, she combines her love of silk and dyes by creating extraordinary fairies, mermaids, and other one-of-a-kind dolls. She has a full line of cloth doll patterns and her work has appeared in books, magazines, and galleries. In demand as a teacher, she travels throughout the world. She is the author of *Creative Cloth Doll Making* (Rockport 2003).